REFLECTIONS

The First Eighty-Six Years

PAMELA LEE

For Herb,

without whom much of what follows would
never have happened.

Herb Lee

June 5, 1926 – April 6, 2006

Who's Who?

- Pamela: Julia Pamela Cherry Lee, b. 26 November, 1930
- Julia Wyche: Pamela's mother, Julia Wyche Allen, m. Hix Cherry, 31 December 1925
- Hix: Pamela's father, William Hix Cherry
- Bill: Pamela's brother, William Hix Cherry, Jr; Bob and Charles Cherry, Bill's sons
- Herb: Pamela's husband, Herbert Martin Lee, Jr, m. 14 March, 1953
- Lisa: Pamela Elisabeth Lee, daughter of Pamela and Herb, married
- Pat: Patrick Sullivan, 1 April, 1989
- Hillary: Hillary Susan Lee, daughter of Pamela and Herb, married:
- Gray: Gray Safford, 14 July, 1990
- Dan: Daniel Safford, son of Hillary and Gray, b. 10 March, 1992
- Susan: Susan Safford, daughter of Hillary and Gray, b. 11 February, 1994
- Dr.. Joseph Augustus Allen: Pamela's maternal grandfather
- Pamela Wyche Allen: Pamela's maternal grandmother
- Rev. William Samuel Coke Cherry, Pamela's paternal grandfather
- Julia Allen Hix, Pamela's paternal grandmother

- Julia Mabel Cherry, Hugh Allen Cherry, Jane Estelle Cherry Lawing: Hix Cherry's siblings
- Johanna and Allen Cherry: children of Hugh and Dorothy Cherry
- Veatrice/Nana: Herb's mother, Veatrice Wilson Lee
- Ruthie Ledford, Pamela's childhood friend
- Shin Tanaka, adopted friend of the Cherry family
- Arthur Garceau, another adopted family member
- Forrest Hedden: married Pamela and Herb
- Helen Sharpe: traveling companion of Pamela, early and late
- Joy Ballinger: climbing/backpacking companion
- Susan Baldwin: sometime partner of Bill, "sister" of Pamela, travel sponsor and companion
- Suzan Dentry: downsizer extraordinaire, tennis/running buddy
- Weez: Louise Decker, owner of a ski shop in Lambertville, N.J.
- Nancy Strickland: fellow skier/traveler through the years

Chronology

- 1930-1935 Bahama, **North Carolina**
- 1945 N.C. to California with Ledfords
- 1935-1952 Durham, N.C., DHS, Duke University
- 1951 Methodist Caravan working summer
  followed by European Grand Tour
- 1952-1953 Columbia U, New York City
- 1953 marriage and cross-country honeymoon
- 1953-1954 Honolulu, **Hawaii**; Feb. 28 birth of Lisa
- 1955 Durham, N.C.; Oct. 11 birth of Hillary
- 1955 Liverpool, N.Y.
- 1956-1957 Ankara, **Turkey** (Herb in Dyarbakir)
- 1957-1963 Miami, Fla.; Pamela teaches English at
  SW Miami High
- 1963-1967 Bremerton, Wash.
- 1967-1972 Naples (Pozzuoli), **Italy**
- 1973-1978 Long Island, N.Y., law librarian for
  Lauterstein and Lauterstein; Herb in S.C.
- 1978-1979 Abdanan, **Iran**

- 1979-1980 Buenos Aires (Moreno) **Argentina**; early 80's Pat & Herb at Briarcliff in Cockeysville, Md.; Pam to Cedar Tree EST; Suzan changes my life
- 1983 Maryland Marathon
- 1987 Hillary & Gray buy old house, barn, acreage at Lockatong, Lambertville, N.J.
- 1989 Lisa's & Pat's wedding at Painted Desert, Calif.
- 1990 Hillary's & Gray's garden wedding at Louise's. New Hope, Penn.; Jim B
- 1991 New York Marathon
- 1991 Pam with H & G on Lockatong, Lambertville, N.J.
- 1992 birth of Daniel March 10
- 1994 birth of Susan Feb 11; Pam moves in with LL & Pat in Millington, N.J.
- 1999 Pam travels in **India, Nepal, and Tibet**
- 2000 Pam buys home she names "Turnup" in Abington, Penn.
- 2001 Philadelphia Marathon
- 2002 Pam's 50th reunion; publication of *Vultures, Mold, and Other Delights*
- 2003 H & G; D & S move to **Germany**; Pam visits

- 2005 Pam and Herb to Sierra Vista, **Arizona** to live with LL & Pat
- 2006 Pam radiation and chemo; Gamma Knife surgery for acoustic neuroma; Herb's suicide
- 2008 Pam & Nan to Kenya; Bill's death in November
- 2011 Nan/Pam: SW Circuit, Guatemala, Kenya, Gallapagos/Machu Picchu
- 2011 LL & Pat move up Ramsey Canyon; Pam to Mountain View Gardens
- 2013 after Stretto tour, Hillary/Pam enjoy nostalgia trip to Italy
- 2015 March, Pamela wins 1st & 2nd place in Cochise Poetry Competition
- 2015 December, debut of *Imagine,* Sky Island UU poetry anthology
- 2016 creating *Reflections*

Table of Contents

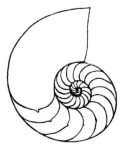

Family Matters

Baby on Board

I've crossed the United States at least five times. My first transcontinental road trip was *in utero*. I don't remember much about that one.

In the summer of 1930, Mother and Daddy and four fellow school teachers set out from North Carolina for California in two touring cars. In all those miles they encountered only one paved road. They crossed the Rockies, visited the Grand Canyon, Yosemite and Yellowstone. Not realizing how balmy summer days can turn frigid at night in the desert, they nearly froze sleeping outdoors in The Painted Desert. Mother said the only thing she didn't do that she might have done, had she not been pregnant, was ride a mule down Bright Angel Trail at the Grand Canyon.

Only Mother and Daddy and Perry (the other driver) knew Mother was expecting. When I appeared in November, everyone thought she must have adopted me. In those days no one spoke about

Lee

"expecting;" there were no maternity clothes, and mothers-to-be disguised their baby bumps. It was as if carrying a child were somehow shameful or embarrassing. Perhaps because the appearance of a baby implied sex? Wonder what that generation would have made of Demi Moore's beautiful gravid belly displayed on the cover of *Vanity Fair*.

A Little Family History

My mother, Julia Wyche Allen, was an only child – a lonely only child. She was valedictorian of her high school graduating class, a class of two. New London was a very small town. So off she went to Louisburg College at age sixteen where she says she cried from September through Thanksgiving.

Mother was so naïve that when college girls giggled about where babies came from, Mother thought them silly. She KNEW where babies came from. They came from the little black satchel which her father, the country doctor, took with him on his calls whenever there was a new baby.

How her father became a doctor is another story. Joseph Augustus Allen was born to a big farming family in Yadkin County, North Carolina. As a child, Joseph contracted rheumatic fever, and his older brother – whose name really was Solomon – wisely determined that Joseph would not be strong enough for farm work. Thus Joseph was the only one of his generation to get an education. He taught in a one-room schoolhouse to earn money for medical school.

Upon graduation from Richmond Medical School, young Dr. Allen was hired by Dr. Robert Henry Wyche to take over Dr. Wyche's medical practice. The Wyches were aristocracy compared to the farmers; they could trace their lineage to Charlemagne. Dr. Wyche's daughter, Pamela (pronounced Pa ME la), even went to college (Normal School), and Dr. Wyche would rather spend his time reading his Old Testament in Greek than dispensing pills and salves.

It didn't take long for the younger doctor to fall in love with the older doctor's daughter, and so they were married. Julia Wyche, their only child and my mother, was born in 1904.

When Mother was eighteen, she transferred from Louisburg College to Duke University, and, determined to become a medical missionary, she majored in sciences. A college graduate before she was twenty, Mother felt she should work a while to earn the money for medical school rather than burden her country doctor father – who often got paid in butter and eggs or the occasional country ham.

Mother had agreed to a high school teaching position, but her cousin Bettie intervened, "Julia, you can't do that! There will be high school boys in your classes both bigger and older than you!" Hix Cherry to the rescue. My father-to-be had just finished his Masters' and was the newly assigned principal of a consolidated school in Bahama, North Carolina. Hix offered Julia a position as a first grade teacher, and she accepted. They were married that New Year's Eve.

"For Mother, no medical school, no going to China as a missionary, no "unbinding the feet of Mai Ling." Instead, teaching children to read and write. And eventually, motherhood. Because Mother was anemic it took my parents six years to conceive me.

Was ever a child so welcome! Awaiting my appearance were two eager parents, two complete sets of grandparents for whom I would be the first

Lee

grandchild, two doting childless aunts, even a living ninety-six-year-old great grandfather.

Not only that, but home was a "teacherage," a big sort of boarding house where most of the teachers for the consolidated school lived – many of them maiden ladies who would vie for the privilege of taking care of Baby Pam.

It was an auspicious beginning to what has been and still is a wonderful life.

A Warm Childhood Memory

I grew up in the segregated South. North Carolina may have been one of the more progressive, more enlightened Southern states, but segregation was strictly the rule even if it was not blatant.

Segregation was so subtle, so far from my consciousness, that on my first visit to New York City in 1947 as a high school junior and delegate to the Columbia Scholastic Press Association – our high school newspaper, *Hi-Rocket*, always won a medalist rating – when a reporter asked me how many high schools there were in Durham, I answered, "Just one." "Don't you mean two?" she asked. That's how oblivious I had been.

Not only that, although I hate to admit it (there's no easy way to put this), my father was a racist. Prejudice was one of those topics like politics or religion which he and I learned to avoid. I have long since forgiven him. After all, he was a product

Lee

of his Time and of his Place; he could hardly have been otherwise.

In Durham we lived on the corner 6th and B. B was a busy street, a few blocks south of the black neighborhood called Haiti (pronounced HAY tye), and a few blocks north of 9th Street where there was what today we would call a strip mall. Oh! The delicious, fresh, warm, greasy doughnuts we would get from Whitman's Bakery on 9th Street and devour on our way to the library at Erwin Mills to check out the next Nancy Drew!

Naturally, black folks would often pass our house on their way to shop on 9th Street. Ours was a big old two-story frame house, and we rented the side apartment. (The rent helped in those post-Depression years.) In the big back yard one of our renters had constructed a swing set and bars made from sawed-off telephone poles run through with two-inch pipes.

One day, when playmates Ellen and Betty Sue were nowhere to be found, and a little black boy was passing by on his way to 9th Street, I invited him to play with me. I don't remember whether he hesitated or not. (Had he been older he certainly would have!) Anyway, he accepted my invitation, and we were taking turns rolling over those bars and trying to chin ourselves when my mother – bless her – brought us lemonade and cookies.

I don't know how many years went by before I realized what a brave gesture that was.

Night Fishing

I remember, I remember

Night fishing with my father:

A bridge with arches that made full circles in the water,

The smell of shrimp for bait,

The lappings of salty wavelets against the boat,

How the lantern hissed, how the light underlit our faces,

How the moonlight on the river – indeed,

How all light radiated and converged on us,

The center of the universe.

Childhood Discipline

My father never hit me. Well, once he did backhand me in the car – no doubt for my smart mouth or for talking back. I remember not only being hurt but being astonished. And I think he truly regretted it.

Mother's technique, when Bill or I needed a reminder, was two vigorous swats on the backside. Far more effective was her look of disapproval if we erred. We both hated to disappoint her.

My worst punishment was not a spanking, not anything physical. I was instructed to go to the new neighbor's, three houses down, and apologize. Miss White, the nosy neighbor next door, had informed Mother she had seen me sticking out my tongue at the new neighbor as she walked by. (People did much more walking in those days.)

Oh! the agony, the dread, the embarrassment, the chagrin! I would have much preferred three spankings to that errand. The longer I postponed the visit, the more formidably it loomed. Eventually, head hanging, I got my feet to shuffle in the right direction. "What's the worst that can happen?" I asked.

Well, the new neighbor was most gracious – and likely amused – in accepting my apology. In fact, she gave me a nickel to reward my belated manners.

That experience contained a valuable life lesson: the dread is usually much worse than the deed. Nike's motto, "JUST DO IT" is good advice.

Saturday Movies

Recently, before I came across the playbill, I was trying to remember the name of the older, more elegant movie theater in Durham. It was a handsome venue, almost an opera house, and in 1934 my mother had seen Katharine Cornell, Basil Rathbone, and Orson Welles there in a live performance of "The Barretts of Wimpole Street."

I tried Corinthian and Criterion and knew they weren't right. In the wee hours on Sunday morning the memory surfaced; it was the Carolina Theater. Funny how memory works, I had been close; the capital C, the r, and the n were present in all three names.

There was a third movie theater in town whose marquee officially read "Uptown Theater" but which would be forever known as "The Rommel Theater" after "The Desert Fox" ran there for what seemed forever.

Lee

But it was the "Center" theater that was an institution in my childhood. Saturday matinée admission was just a dime – albeit that ten cents plus a nickel for a big Milky Way or a box of Milk Duds – consumed a considerable portion of my twenty-five-cent allowance.

But what a bargain! There were always several black and white short comedies (remember Edgar Kennedy?), at least two animated cartoons and always a Frank Buck adventure or a Perils of Pauline serial (to entice us to come back next week to see what happened) – all before the feature. Eddie Ford played rousing music on the magnificent Center Theater Wurlitzer organ, and often there were ticket-number-drawing prizes awarded on the small apron stage. Once I won a pair of roller skates! (There followed a period when my knees were rarely free of scabs or bruises.)

A parent may have dropped us off, but we probably took the bus home – for another nickel.

CAROLINA THEATRE

DURHAM, N. C. · NOBLE ARNOLD, Resident Manager

Wednesday Night, May 2nd, 1934

"Childe Roland to the Dark Tower came . . . "—King Lear

KATHARINE CORNELL

presents

"THE BARRETTS OF WIMPOLE STREET"

by Rudolf Besier

WITH

BASIL RATHBONE

Staged by Guthrie McClintic
Setting and costumes designed by Jo Mielziner

CAUTION: Professionals and amateurs hereby are warned that "The Barretts of Wimpole Street," being fully protected under the copyright laws of the United States of America, the British Empire, including the Dominion of Canada and all other countries of the Copyright Union, is subject to royalty. All rights, including professional, amateur, motion pictures, recitations, public readings, radio broadcasting and the rights of translation into foreign languages are strictly reserved. All inquiries regarding this play should be addressed to Miss Cornell.

THE CAST
(In order of appearance)

DOCTOR CHAMBERS	DAVID GLASSFORD
ELIZABETH BARRETT MOULTON-BARRETT	KATHARINE CORNELL
WILSON	BRENDA FORBES
HENRIETTA MOULTON-BARRETT	HELEN WALPOLE
ARABEL MOULTON-BARRETT	PAMELA SIMPSON
OCTAVIUS MOULTON-BARRETT	ORSON WELLES
SEPTIMUS MOULTON-BARRETT	IRVING MORROW
ALFRED MOULTON-BARRETT	CHARLES BROKAW
CHARLES MOULTON-BARRETT	LATHROP MITCHELL
HENRY MOULTON-BARRETT	REYNOLDS EVANS
GEORGE MOULTON-BARRETT	GEORGE MACREADY
EDWARD MOULTON-BARRETT	CHARLES WALDRON
BELLA HEDLEY	MARGOT STEVENSON
HENRY BEVAN	JOHN HOYSRADT
ROBERT BROWNING	BASIL RATHBONE
DOCTOR FORD-WATERLOW	A. P. KAYE
CAPTAIN SURTEES COOK	FRANCIS MORAN
FLUSH	FLUSH

This comedy was played in Elizabeth Barrett's bed-sitting room at 50, Wimpole Street, London, in 1845.

SCENES

ACT I: Scene 1—The evening of the 19th of May
        2—The afternoon of the following day

INTERMISSION: 5 MINUTES

ACT II: Three months later

INTERMISSION: 9 MINUTES

ACT III: Scene 1—Some weeks later
          2—The following week
(During Scene 2 the lights will be lowered to denote the passing of a few hours.)

Special period furniture by Hampton Shops. Other furnishings by William Birns and Lavezzo Brothers. Costumes and uniforms executed by Helene Pons Studio. Production built by T. B. McDonald Construction Co.; painted by Robert Bergman Studios. Electrical equipment by Century Lighting Company. Shoes by I. Miller & Sons, Inc. Wigs by A. Barris.

To aid The Actors' Fund of America, Miss Cornell makes a charge of fifty cents for her autographed photograph. The entire sum is given to the Fund.

FOR MISS CORNELL:

General Representative	Gertrude Macy
Company Manager	Allan Attwater
Technical Director	Kate Drain Lawson
Stage Manager	James Vincent
Assistant Stage Manager	Robert Champlain
Assistant in Advance	Morton Nathanson
Advance Representative	Ray Henderson

Thursday - Friday - Saturday, May 3rd - 4 - 5

George White's "SCANDALS"

WITH

Rudy Vallee—Alice Faye
Jimmy Durante—Cliff Edwards—Geo. White

HUNT PRINTING CO., DURHAM, N. C.

35

Lee

Reflections on an Old Spanish Ballad

You know how a tune can get stuck in your head, and cycle continually? Well, lately the song that keeps playing and replaying for me is one I learned in grammar school with Miss Blue, the music teacher who came once a week. I could remember most of the words; a computer search filled them out. It goes like this:

Soft o'er the fountain
Ling'ring falls the southern moon.
Far o'er the mountain
Breaks the day too soon!

In thy dark eyes' splendor
Where the warm light loves to dwell,
Weary looks yet tender
Speak their fond farewell.
    Nita, Juanita!
    Ask thy soul if we should part.
    Nita, Juanita,
    Lean thou on my heart.

When I learned that song – in fourth grade? at age nine? – there was the kinesthetic pleasure of singing. But, at the time, it was pure rote memorization with little or no thought of what the words were saying. Now, as I think about them, I realize how sad they are: lovers having to part at daybreak, a poignant parallel to *Romeo and Juliet*. And we know how *that* turns out.

So I ponder: would we rather be moved or amused? Laughter is wonderful; certainly we all need it, but laughter is fleeting. Sad songs linger, and they evoke in us feelings of empathy and compassion. Not a bad thing. So, go ahead. Sing me sad songs.

Lee

Blackie Was a Good Dog

"Will-YUM!" Mother yelled from the front
porch. (Actually Mother rarely if ever raised her
voice.) Then quietly murmured to herself, "If he isn't
hurt, I'm going to kill him!" Bill was late coming
home from his evening paper route.

Only Mother called him William; to everyone
else my five years younger brother was Bill. Bill and
Blackie did eventually show up for supper, neither of
them hurt, and Mother didn't even spank him.
Maybe he was getting too old for that.

I've no recollection of how Blackie came to be
in the family. He was all sorts of mix, looking to be
mostly setter with his wavy black coat and his lean
but sturdy body. Probably Daddy thought he might
become a good hunting dog. No such luck. Blackie
turned out to be gun shy. (Maybe, like the rest of the
family, he had no heart for hunting.)

But that dog could sing! Whenever Bill was
banished from the house to the back yard to

practice his trumpet, Blackie would accompany him with punctuated yips and yowls. Apparently, Blackie wasn't howling from discomfort at my brother's learning efforts; he never ran away from the noise. Bill eventually became proficient enough to play trumpet in both the high school and university marching bands. (Premier seats for lots of sports!)

Blackie could tell time. He knew exactly when I had to leave for high school in the morning and would accompany me clear across the university campus to the downtown all-white high school.

After escorting me to Durham High, Blackie would wait until the bell rang before heading back across busy streets and the Duke campus in time to walk with my brother to E. K. Poe Junior High school on the other side of town. I don't know what Blackie did in the meantime, but when school was over he knew when to meet Bill to accompany him on his evening paper route.

Perhaps some dark-skinned youngster, fearful of a big, black, unchained dog, threw a stone. For whatever reason Blackie began barking at Negroes passing by his yard. There were complaints. This was long before leash laws, and my father couldn't bear the thought of confining or chaining a dog who had always run free. So Daddy explained to my brother that he would find Blackie a good home in the country where Blackie could play with other dogs and chase rabbits.

Bill understood and was brave. Through the tears he tried not to shed, Bill's only comment was, "Blackie was a good dog."

Cat Tales

There were always cats. The cats of our childhood never knew about vets, kitty litter, or special cat food. They ate what we ate – green beans and all. And they were indoor-outdoor creatures.

Tommy (such an imaginative name!) was a great, gray tabby, white-chested, white-footed tomcat. He must have been an alpha male; he traveled contentedly with us the hundred miles between Durham and New London several times a year, was at home in both locales, and never had a mark on him. When elderly and somewhat crotchety I watched him enter a neighbor baby's playpen and submit to the the baby's delighted tail-, whisker-, and ear-pulling without a complaint; he just walked off when he'd had enough. Finally he just walked off.

When I was in college, still living at home, my then-boyfriend and medical student Bill Anderson, brought me a kitten in a paper bag – literally. As he

Lee

was all black – the cat, not Bill – I named him Mephistopheles, but called him Fisty. In 1950, cats could still come and go, and Fisty came and went as he pleased. He *would* seek refuge when blue jays would dive-bomb him on the patio. And when there was a heavy rain or snowstorm, he'd meow beneath my bedroom window to be let in. After I opened the window and the screen, he would have to make a tremendous leap to just manage to get his front paws on the windowsill after which I could haul him in.

Fisty continued to live with Mother and Daddy after I moved on – to graduate school, then marriage and family. On return visits I learned that there were several Fisty lookalikes in the West Durham neighborhood.

Daisy, the girls' kitten in Miami was a teenager herself. Lisa and Hillary watched Daisy give birth to Smokey and Tarbaby.

Isolde was Lisa's cat at Bank Street in NYC. That cat would try valiantly to explain to me how to get into the apartment when Lisa wasn't home.

Isolde and Chance, who belonged to Lisa's apartment-mate, Nancy Press, were wont to run thunder races down the fifth-floor apartment's hardwood hall.

The barn manager didn't want the mostly-Maltese cat at Centenary College where Hillary was teaching Equitation. So Hillary took her home on approval. Gray named her Yardley for the Little Grey Nuns of Yardley. She often slept on my bed in the upstairs back bedroom at Lockatrong. Even sound asleep she could hear the refrigerator open and would race downstairs in hopes cheese might be forthcoming. And she stole olives!

Grey wept unabashedly as he held her in her favorite blanket when she had to be put down. She is buried near the back of the Yard Road property, her grave decorated with shells and pretty stones by Daniel and Susan.

Slow Talent and Daring Amelia moved with Hillary, Gray, Daniel, and Susan from Abington, Pennsylvania to Germany! There were several tense days while Talent went missing, but he eventually

Lee

found his way back to his new home. When Gray's Germany tour was over, Talent and Amelia stayed in Germany where they found new, happy homes with delighted owners.

Once back in Abington, Susan and Daniel adopted Jamarcus, a tabby, and all-black Ninja. When the two would tussle, Ninja was the quicker, but Jamarcus outweighed him, so they were pretty evenly matched. One Christmas, Ninja wore himself out tirelessly batting and swinging from a cat toy hung from a door frame. (And wore us out laughing.) Ninja has a strange habit of drowning little toy animals, paper towels, and tissues in his water bowl. Never leave an open box of Kleenex where he can find it! Now that the kids have moved on, Ninja has become Hillary's cat. He is a particular favorite of all who know him.

When Herb and I lived in Argentina, I brought home yet another little black kitten. (The guys at the coal and gas place where I went to pick up a propane tank promised to kill it if I didn't take her.) I called her Carboncita – "little lump of coal." Before long, she began surprising Herb and me by jumping onto our bed early in the morning before we were up. Now that kitchen door to the outside was a heavy metal one, so I assumed one of the dogs had managed to open it. That is, until one day when I watched that little cat climb to the top of the wall. over the outside laundry sink, launch herself in the air, and catch the door handle on her way down.

In my opinion, the best-named cats were Lisa's Basil and Coriander. Basil's replacement, Cinco de Mayo (who clearly chose Lisa) and Coriander traveled by plane from New Jersey to Arizona, accompanied by an Air France friend of Lisa's.

While we lived on Bannock Street in Sierra Vista, Corrie almost always slept on my bed – often *under* the covers. I was so distraught when she died that Lisa finally yelled at me: "Get your own cat!"

So I did. When there wasn't a kitten to be found at the shelters, Lisa and I answered an ad and went way out in the country where we got first pick of a litter. The calico kitten I named Bouquet came to live with me when she was just six weeks old. Her father was probably feral, which would account for her pervasive skittishness. Bouquet moved with me to Mountain View Gardens in 2011. I'm delighted she likes to sleep with me. Her quirk? She steals the paper clips I use as bookmarks and hides them in the bedclothes.

Some cats are finicky eaters. Bouquet is one. I have offered her clams, salmon, tilapia, and bacon – all of which she sniffs and refuses. She even seems to be putting her paws on her hips and saying indignantly, "Where's my Kibble?"

When Cinco de Mayo died, Lisa was in the market for another cat, so she and I went cat shopping. Pat's only caveat on our choice was that it be a domestic short-hair. Wouldn't you know; the adolescent cat Lisa and I fell in love with was most likely a Maine Coon, definitely a long-hair. Said Lisa, "We have to call Pat." She did, Pat came, and it was love at first sight for him also.

We never understood why anyone would abandon such a handsome, valuable cat, but someone had thoughtfully left this one at the Pepsi bottling plant just across the street from the old shelter. Which is how Pepsi got his name.

At their Ramsey Canyon place Pat has constructed an elaborate several-story cat aviary for Pepsi and Pardo with a swinging door they can go through from the dining room. Now those cats can have some outdoor time safe from coyotes, owls, and hawks. And the local birds are safe from the cats.

Lee

Aunt Estelle

My grandmother Cherry had picked out marriage partners for all four of her children, pairing them with the four Hubbards, offspring of her best friend.

Well, Mabel, the eldest, chose not to marry at all and left the country to become a missionary in Korea.

Hix, my father, had no interest in Ruth Hubbard and married my mother instead.

Hugh, the third child, thumbed his nose at his Methodist upbringing and married a woman he had known only a few days and she a Catholic.

Estelle, the baby, did manage to become engaged to Paul Hubbard, but he jilted her and married a woman he met while away on a job. Paul couldn't face Estelle and sent his bride to collect the engagement ring.

Estelle was a beautiful young woman with wavy hair and blue eyes. And she had style; I always picture her in an elegant garden party hat. But I think that broken engagement left her with a bitter streak.

She became a school teacher and married the most eligible bachelor in Long Creek where she went to teach. Frank Lawing had a degree from NC State, but he didn't use it as proprietor of the local general store and gas station.

Eventually Estelle persuaded Frank to move to High Point where she continued to teach – for forty or more years – while Frank worked at a number of odd jobs. He was a good-looking man and a good one, but he always struck me as something of a milquetoast.

Estelle, on the other hand, thrived in the city. They had no children, but she was active in church and clubs. More significantly, she began dabbling in real estate, buying small houses to renovate and rent. That sideline eventually made her a wealthy woman.

The bitterness I mentioned earlier manifested itself in Estelle's jealousy toward my mother – one who had children when she didn't. Estelle could be verbally cruel. When her feelings were hurt, Mother simply turned the other cheek.

Lacking children of her own, Estelle was more than generous with her four nieces and nephews: me and my brother Bill, and Uncle Hugh's children, Johanna and Allen.

As the oldest of the four (and the most attentive) I became her late-in-life travel companion and eventually her caretaker and executor. She lived to be one hundred six.

Cousins

Mother had fifty-two first cousins whom she could name! When the Allens got together at Great Aunt Rose's in Yadkin County, so many relatives would turn up they had to erect bleachers so everyone could be seen in the picture. Turner Family Reunions were almost as numerous. Even Protestants had big families back then when workers were needed on the farms.

What a shift! My brother Bill and I have only two first cousins. Mother was an only child so none there. Neither of Daddy's two sisters had children, but Uncle Hugh and Aunt Dot copied Mother and Daddy and had first a girl, Johanna, then a boy, Allen, our only first cousins.

Most of the Cherrys were Methodist, Papa Cherry a preacher, Aunt Mabel a missionary in Korea. Uncle Hugh's family were Catholic since Aunt Dot was. Most of us lived in North Carolina; Uncle Hugh and his family lived in Baltimore.

Lee

Jo and Allen grew up, went to college, married their high school sweethearts and settled close to home in Baltimore. Allen taught vocational classes in high school. Jo would have been an excellent teacher but Jerry, her up-and-coming husband with Mars Markets, didn't want his wife to work. Jo and Jerry had two girls, Dee Dee (for grandmother Dorothy) and Cherry Ann. Allen and Betty had Leona and Todd. They were a close-knit family, and they lived in Baltimore, but we did get to see them summers when they would vacation at Aunt Mabel's cottage at Lake Junaluska.

Through the years, I had lived in Turkey, Iran, Italy, and Argentina and had traveled wherever and whenever I could, before fate settled Herb in Maryland to do engineering writing. As Jo lived close by for the first time, I invited her to lunch at our apartment in Cockeysville, Maryland. At some juncture Jo asked me, "How on earth could you stand it, being so far away from home for so long?"

I bit my tongue and did not voice my thought: "How could *you* stand it, living all your life in one place?"

It's a long, sad story, but Jo and Allen became estranged and spent their later years not speaking to each other. (It made me appreciate my brother Bill and our excellent relationship.)

The second and third generations have been more friendly, the family feud mere history when they came together in North Carolina for Aunt Estelle's One Hundredth Birthday celebration.

The Greely Place

My grandfather, the country doctor, probably planted the first tree farm in North Carolina. In 1916 Granddaddy bought an old farm in Harris Township, not far from his New London home in Stanly County. And in 1937 he had twenty-five acres of it planted in Loblolly pines. The Longleaf pine is the state tree.

Grandaddy probably harvested at least one lumber cutting before Mother inherited the property. She continued the reforestation project with the assistance of David Long, then the County Agricultural Agent.

Mother earned income from several cuttings before she bequeathed the Greely Place to me. To keep matters equitable, Bill got a property on the coast as he liked to sail.

In 1979 David Long asked to buy a seven-acre piece for a home for the family. He would eventually purchase a second plot, one for each of his sons Brian and Wesley.

I was infuriated when I discovered I couldn't sell a piece of my own property without Herb's signature! What did *he* have to do with it?

Through the years David and Mother became good friends. For me he was both friend and caretaker for The Greely Place while I lived far away. He would monitor when I should thin-cut and harvest – in exchange for exclusive bow-hunting rights for him and the boys. Turkeys, certainly. Maybe deer.

It was David who told me the place was known locally as "Doctor's Mountain." Eventually, David and his wife Pam would become owners of the entire almost 100 acres, Granddaddy's mountain and all.

The Greely Place is nostalgic for me. It was a wonderful site for blackberry-picking with my grandfather.

Lee

Me and Br'er Rabbit

Deems, bless him,

brought me a basketful

of big, beautiful, cultivated blackberries

from Talbot's Farm.

He may have heard me voice my frustration

at jogging past a patch on Padonia every day

with no time to stop and pick.

Or perhaps the poor man was embarrassed

at having to pause while his tennis partner

compulsively devoured the fruit of the spindly volunteers

down by the courts.

Reflections

I told him I just loved berries –

to explain my evident rapture.

Did not tell him

I was simply trying to recapture my childhood:

...sensing on my back an earlier July sun,

one that beat down on the briar patch at the Greely Place,

on my grandfather and me with our lard cans clinking,

hearing the first berries plink into the pails,

the lazy buzz of cicadas,

a cow lowing in the next pasture,

recalling the powdery beige dust that coated everything,

the keen scent of the kerosene-soaked rags we wore

on wrists and ankles as barriers to bugs.

Lee

Now picturing Mima and Mildred

– Mildred with her pale, pink palms –

back in the kitchen with the Mason jars

and jelly glasses boiling,

the white mountains of sugar weighed and measured....

I was a Time-traveler, Deems,

a far piece from the tennis courts at Briarcliff East,

caught up in the blackberry briars of my youth –

without the chiggers!

The berries were wonderful.

Then as now.

About Herb

Herbert Martin Lee, Jr. Here I confess I always preferred his middle name; nevertheless, he was Herb, my husband of fifty-two years – off and on. Mostly on.

Our lifestyle dictated much of the "off." Herb's engineering assignments would take him away for days, weeks, or even months at a time – on sea trials or as in Turkey when he was in Diyarbakır and I wasn't allowed to accompany him.

We were divorced in 1963 but remarried two months later. In the later years of our marriage we chose to live separately.

Herb had his faults. (Don't we all! I shan't enumerate my own here.) Looking back, I have two complaints: the primary one was Herb's unwillingness to communicate. We never managed to talk about problems; we just ignored them until they lost importance, and somehow they did.

Lee

The second issue was his lack of overt affection – no spontaneous hugs, hand-holding, nuzzling, or secret, knowing smiles. I didn't doubt his love; I just would have enjoyed more expression of it.

Our sex life was a whole other thing. It was probably that powerful attraction that made us work as a couple, because Herb and I were polar personalities. It was more than a left brain/right brain difference, Engineer v. English major. Herb was by nature a loner. While I liked time alone, I was more gregarious and enjoyed social exchange. His thinking was linear; mine was more random. I was a liberal Democrat, and he was a *Republican*, for God's sake! We probably canceled each other's votes in every national election. My first vote, after I became twenty-one, was for Adlai Stevenson.

It may have been turbulent, but ours was a good marriage. Although Herb hadn't wanted to marry, he was a good husband. And although he *really* didn't want to have children – I realized later that he was fearful of passing on the ataxia genes –

we had two. And he was an excellent parent. He was perhaps too stern and I too passive. But it was Herb who suggested the girls take art lessons, learn horseback riding, get ballet training, and Herb who encouraged them to deal with challenges.

For instance: during one brief residence on Long Island, Herb registered nine-year-old Lisa in astronomy and rocks-and-minerals courses at the Hayden Planetarium and Museum of Natural History.

Then he taught her how to take the Long Island Rail Road into Manhattan and which subways to take in the City. Once, a LIRR conductor, realizing she was traveling alone, took her to the front car where the engineer let her blow the whistle.

Hillary's challenge was to walk from the duplex on 76th Street to Coral Gables, there to buy bedding of her choice.

Not only did Herb enlarge the girls' lives, he vastly enriched my own. Many, perhaps most of the accomplishments I am proudest of in my life were instigated by Herb.

Lee

Okay, I was a good swimmer before Herb and I met. In fact, I had earned my Red Cross Water Safety Instructor credentials senior year at Duke. It was Suzan who got me into running after I turned fifty, and the stint at teaching was my choice.

But it was Herb who introduced me to skiing, to SCUBA-diving, to back-packing, to mountain-climbing, he who was responsible for my becoming a private pilot. That's not to mention all the far-ranging travel he provided or supported.

Being in love, living abroad, getting to travel extensively, and having two wonderful daughters together? What's not to like!

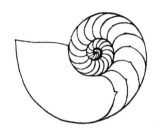

School Days

Lee

Things Come in Threes

Have you ever noticed how things seem to come in threes? Especially deaths. At Mountain View Gardens, first there was Donna, then Sherman. For me, the third was Jimmy Heldman, a high school classmate.

I learned of Jimmy's death through one of the emails fellow classmate Laurie Belvin Franklin sends with updates concerning our Durham High School Class of 1948.

He may have called himself Jim, but for me he will forever be Jimmy, the Darcy to my Elizabeth in *Pride and Prejudice.* And how being in that Senior Play changed his life!

After we graduated high school, I lived at home and went to Duke, my parents' alma mater; Jimmy traveled eleven miles down the road to the University of North Carolina at Chapel Hill. We both majored in English. Playing Darcy in high school was the trigger for Jim's fascination with Jane Austen such that he became a Jane Austen scholar with several publications to his credit. At one time he was vice-president of the International Jane Austen Society.

Nor did Jimmy lose his love of theater. After a Master's in Drama he was a one-man theater department at Roanoke College for two years. He earned his PhD in English at UNC after which he taught at several universities, eventually becoming head of the English department at Western Kentucky University at Bowling Green. All the while he was active in professional, college, and community theater. And all – or at least partly – because of a high school play.

Besides Jimmy's successes, of that *Pride and Prejudice* cast, Bobby Evans (Mr. Bennet) became a Rhodes scholar and understudy to Edward R. Murrow, and Mary Ann Harrell (Mrs. Bennet) wound up with her name on the masthead of *The National Geographic*. Not too shabby for a class of just over two hundred members, eh?

But events don't necessarily come in threes – at least no more often than they occur singly or in pairs. We are just conditioned to remember things in threes, and there's a reason.

Long before there was the written word, history was oral, the province of story-tellers and minstrels. Those bards of old understood that people were more likely to remember matters if they were sung or recited in small groups of three.

The Greek orators certainly were aware of the rule of three, as were the Romans. Caesar's *veni vidi vinci* (I came; I saw; I conquered) is surely one of the world's most famous Latin quotations.

Rules of rhetoric were certainly familiar to Abraham Lincoln. One has only to recall the Gettysburg Address. Its mere two hundred seventy-two words incorporate two such 'periods':

"...we cannot dedicate, we cannot consecrate, we cannot hallow this ground."

Lee

and, "...that government of the people, by the people, for the people shall not perish from the earth."

When two is company, three may be a crowd, but when writing or communicating, Jimmy would have known how powerful three can be.

Maiden Ladies

What became of all those maiden ladies that peopled my childhood and adolescence? Single females nowadays are career women, often with power jobs and big responsibilities. No stigma such as "spinster" or "old maid" attached.

Most of my teachers were unmarried older women. There was the warm giant Mamie Mansfield (sixth grade) who once trusted me with $100 to take to the office. I was especially fond of dotty Miss Hamilton (ninth-grade English) who read *Rostam and Sohrab* to us and, to our everlasting amusement, actually put the spelling words on the blackboard.

In eighth and ninth grades I took Latin under the Dean, the formidable Miss Counselor. That little bit of Latin changed my life. The complex Latin grammar made English grammar such a breeze that I was a whiz at English and wound up majoring in it.

Lee

Miss Blue, the roving grammar school music teacher, who came once a week, taught us songs like "Funiculì, Funiculà" and "Nita, Juanita" which I still remember and could sing for you – if I could still sing.

The most beautiful teacher was Esther Horner, of fourth grade geography. Remember drawing all those maps of the Fertile Crescent and Mesopotamia between the Tigris and Euphrates? Maybe she doesn't count, as she got married.

Eunice Jones was a neighbor as well as my sixth grade English teacher. We kept in touch for years.

In ninth grade Grace Tilley praised my *Ivanhoe* paper contrasting Rebecca and Rowena, and it was she who coached me to winning the recitation medal that year.

In high school there was Marguerite Herr, head of the English department, who terrified almost everybody. A short, corseted, fire-hydrant-shaped, middle-aged woman with a pince nez, she turned out to be a pussycat instead of a tiger to those of us who worked on the school newspaper, the *Hi-Rocket*, under her auspices. She retired after my senior year – along with three other department heads: Pop DeBrunye (Math), 'Fesser Twaddell (Music), and the beloved Miss Maude, vocational arts coordinator. I corresponded with Miss Herr for years.

My Aunt Mabel never married yet lived an interesting life as a missionary in Korea until an evacuation in the thirties. Aunt Estelle got married to Uncle Frank, but as they had no children, she seemed more like one of the maiden ladies.

Perhaps the most colorful old maids were Miss Belle and Miss Ada, the unmarried older sisters of Uncle Frank. They remained in the big house on the family homestead and, despite being quite well-off from cotton, lumber, and tobacco, they never put in electricity, running water, or indoor plumbing!

Another maiden pair of interest were Miss Anne and Miss Olive who lived across the street from my Cherry grandparents in Newton. Whether it

Lee

was Miss Anne or Miss Olive I don't remember, but one of them had a "gentleman caller." (Otherwise, I might have thought in retrospect they were a gay couple: Miss Olive all skinny and stern, Miss Ann big and loud and jolly.) Of an evening Miss Anne, Miss Olive, and the gentleman caller would sit on their porch as my folks sat on theirs, hoping for a breeze.

The adults would exchange casual conversation while the grandchildren were trying vainly to get to sleep in an abominably hot upstairs bedroom, serenaded by noisy cicadas.

I Woke up Singing

This morning it was "When You Wore a Tulip." Of course, I wasn't singing out loud; I rarely do that since my deafness – not even with familiar hymns in church.

But those words and that tune were coming through loud and clear. And they were taking me back to high school days and barbershop quartet singing with Dorothy Leonard. Never mind that we were just a duet and females at that.

Barbershop singing is most often performed by a male quartet or quintet, and Durhan High had a very special one. Guy Fornes, Dwight Carden, Pat Hunt, and Faison Whitaker formed a hillbilly band that enjoyed considerable popularity in town as well as at school talent shows. The guys would show up barefoot (sometimes with a bandaged toe), sporting corncob pipes and large bandana handkerchiefs, dressed in raggedy clothes or too-big bib overalls; and they made music on washboards, little brown jugs, harmonicas, and a home-made string bass as well as vocally.

Dot – Dorothy was always called Dot – and I were just two, but our music definitely belonged in the barbershop genre. Dot had a pure, bell-like soprano voice, and I could sing harmony to almost anything. After we got our act together for a high school talent show, we actually took our show on the road. Civic groups in town would often invite us to be the entertainment at their luncheons.

Dot would wear a frilly, floor-length Southern Belle dress, and I would don dark slacks and a white shirt with a bow tie. I never pasted on or drew on a mustache; a girl needs to retain some degree of femininity.

Our routines almost always began with "For Me and My Gal." Our repertoire included "Daisy, Daisy," "Down by the Old Mill Stream," "In the Evening by the Moonlight," "Show Me the Way to go Home," and, of course, "When You Wore a Tulip":

When you wore a tulip, a sweet yellow tulip
And I wore a big red rose

When you caressed me, 'twas then heaven blessed me
What a blessing, no one knows.
You made life cheery when you called me "Dearie"
'Twas down where the bluegrass grows.
Your lips were sweeter than julip
when you wore that tulip
And I wore a big red rose.

The words were pretty silly – if we ever stopped to think about them – but oh! the harmony was glorious.

First Love

Some of us never get over our first love. I'm one. It happened to me my first year in high school. I was a Sophomore, he a Junior; I was fifteen, he sixteen. We never even had a class together as he was in science, I in arts, but when we passed in the halls I would find myself instantly wet. Hormones and pheromones. Oh my!

Eventually he noticed me – I was hard to miss with the white forelock in my dark hair that had arrived with puberty – and we began dating. We kissed in my living room, we kissed on my front porch swing, we kissed in his car. Once in my back yard I recited to him Elizabeth Barrett Browning's *How Do I Love Thee*. He wanted more than poetry; I said no. And he moved on.

He took a different girl to the prom and gave her a white orchid corsage. Unheard of! I was jealous. When he began dating my best friend, I was furious with both of them.

The following year he asked me out again, and I said yes. This time he asked to wear my silver ring. The teenage me knew I loved him, thought I wanted him for forever, so I said yes and lost my virginity. And he moved on.

When he returned my ring, it smelled of King's Men, his aftershave, and seemed to for years afterward. Although we went to the same university, we probably never saw each other after high school. He was pre-med, I an English major.

And I moved on. I was married with two babies and living half a world away when Mother wrote of his untimely death in an automobile accident. I still wear that silver ring.

My Big Brother Shin

How one thing leads to another. Not long ago I was showing Helen my recently-completed 1,500-piece jigsaw puzzle that had a distinctly Asian feel. We checked; sure enough, the fine print on the box indicated the artist had a Japanese name, Zigen Wanabe. That prompted me to ask, "Did I ever tell you how I acquired a Japanese "big brother"? So I told her:

On a Sunday evening, not long after World War II, my father was outside Duke Memorial Methodist church, smoking a last cigarette before ushering for the evening service, when a Japanese man climbed up the steps, paused, and queried, "Hix?" "Isawo?" my father responded.

My father, Hix Cherry, and Isawo Tanaka had been classmates at Trinity College (soon to become Duke University) in 1919! After graduating from Divinity School, Isawo became a Methodist minister. In 1941, he was living in California with wife Kimi and son Shin. Naturally, after Pearl Harbor, they were interned.

"What are you doing here, Isawo?"

"I'm hoping to see Shin enrolled at Duke."

"Well, I'm sure he'll be accepted, and when he comes, please tell him to consider our home his."

Shin did come, and he did make our home his throughout his seven years of study. We sang in the Duke Memorial choir together; he ate Sunday dinner with us nearly every week. Shin was not only a pre-med student, he was an accomplished classical pianist who found it easier to practice on our Chickering upright than on grand pianos in the Student Union. Thus I acquired a big brother.

Eventually Shin became a prominent internist in the Twin Cities, one well-known for his *pro bono* work. Shin continued with his music – even married his piano teacher. And because he had *two* grand pianos in his gracious home, he was frequently host to visiting professional musicians who would "jam," for their own entertainment there.

Lee

In 1994 Shin and his wife Susie made a trip east. It turned out to be a farewell visit to me and two other east coast friends, mere days before he died. He had undergone a triple by-pass and knew his days were numbered. I am confident that on the train going home to Minneapolis Shin managed to die at a place en route where Susie would be closest to her twin sister.

I attended Shin's memorial service in Minneapolis. Although the church was packed with people, few words were spoken; the program was almost entirely classical music played by his many friends.

Ou Sont Les Neiges
(for Shin)

We were soul-mates once,
Fed each other's dreams,
Sensed a psychic bond we savored
Like persimmons on the tongue.

We were attuned,
Yet, taut as muted viols tuned too high,
We kept contained
Our fierce and fragile harmony.

Our lives diverged.
Yours became heraldic,
A lion, rampant, complete with pride,
Feasting on the meat of life,
A king of creatures, magnificent, admired.

Lee

And I became a ruminant,
Lazily grazing and gazing,
Always in some green and tended pasture,
Feeding on grasses and blossoms,
Wide-eyed, sweet-smelling, bovine.

Of the countless cells of us
That shared that rare and singing
synthesis of souls,
Had we sloughed them all
Before you died?

Art

No, not about art as in paintings, but about Arthur Garceau, my second "big brother." Art became a regular at our Sunday dinners after Shin asked if he could bring a friend and fellow medical student.

Art loved my mother's crumb-top apple pie. One Sunday, as he was leaving, he turned to Mother and said, "Wychie, wish me luck. I'm having a big exam tomorrow." Of course she did, and Art said, "If I ace it, will you make an apple pie for me? And of course he did, and of course she did.

Art earned so many apple pies that Mother claims she helped him earn his Phi Beta Kappa key.

When he graduated from Duke, Art applied to five different medical schools: If I remember correctly, they were Harvard, Johns Hopkins, McGill, Stanford, and Duke. In any case he was accepted at all five. He chose Harvard and remained in Massachusetts, his home state, to practice.

Lee

Art married Davida Gordon, another Duke student. They had three children, one of whom was a daughter named Pamela. Art and Davida eventually divorced, and Art acquired a whole new family when he married Jackie.

I last saw Art at Shin's memorial service in Minneapolis, but we talk on the telephone occasionally. He usually calls me between Thanksgiving and Christmas. If I have a lot to say, I write a letter.

Music, Music, Music

Until I lost my hearing, music played a large part in my life.

In fourth grade I took public school violin lessons with Mr. Pikutis until he went off to war. I never learned to play an instrument, but I did do a lot of singing.

Long before television, the family would sing hymns and golden oldies for entertainment of an evening or a Sunday afternoon. Mother would accompany us on the upright Chickering.

For a while I sang in both the Junior and Senior choirs of Duke Memorial Methodist church. Under Brantley Waton's direction the Senior Choir was accomplished enough to go on a North Carolina tour.

"I Woke up Singing" described barbershop quartet-singing with Dorothy Leonard while in Durham High School. I sang with both the mixed chorus and the girls' chorus in high school. Professor Twadell's choruses always won medalist ratings in

85

state competitions. Although I'm a soprano, in high school I sang alto, because I had range enough and could read music.

The summer of my Junior year, I was one of twelve Methodist Caravaners. We did a lot of singing and harmonizing aboard the *MS Nellie* en route to Europe. In Germany and Austria we shoveled WWII rubble and sang with children and young people in church camps.

In the next chapter, I'll talk about Madrigal singing at Duke.

After we graduated from Duke, dear friend Williams Anderson gave me his guitar. I took it with me to Girl Scout and YWCA summer camps where I was the waterfront director at Crabtree Creek State Park. With the help of a paperback Burl Ives Songbook, I taught myself half a dozen basic cords – enough that I could accompany myself singing folk songs *a la* Joan Baez.

During my semester of graduate school, I was a member of the Columbia University Chorus. The conductor was Jascha Avsholomov. Margo Burrell had a glorious contralto voice, and I was a competent soprano. Both of us were selected to sing with the small antiphonal chorus Jascha needed for some large work, and we were invited to Avsholomov's home to practice. Margo and I became friends on our walks back to Johnson Hall dorm after rehearsals. Almost fifty years later, Margo would be the editor of my poetry collection, *Vultures, Mold, and Other Delights.*

Among the large works the Columbia Chorus performed in concert was Aaron Copland's "In the Beginning," an *a cappella* representation of the creation story. Mr Copland was in the audience for the dress rehearsal; he said he liked our performance better than the only recording available at the time.

While Herb was off in Turkey on that hush-hush assignment, Lisa and I stayed with my parents until I delivered Hillary. During the pregnancy Alan Bone invited me to sing with the Durham Community Chorus. Alan Bone had taught two of my Music Appreciation courses at Duke.

Lee

After a hiatus for marriage, travel, two babies, living in Hawaii and Turkey, and building houses in Florida, I began teaching English in Southwest Miami High School. I was one of the five team teachers responsible for teaching the hundred or so students in our five classes one day of the week. My unit on English Ballads and Folk Songs – which I sang myself – was a big success.

In the years that followed, most of my singing was to myself, although I did coerce daughters Lisa and Hillary to harmonize with me on road trips. One of our favorites was "Jamaica Farewell," another the Kingston Trio's "The Man Who Never Returned (from a ride on the MTA)." (Fortuitously, I once happened on a Kingston Trio concert at Lake Junaluska.) For singing in the car, the girls christened themselves "The Trapped Family Singers."

There was wonderful group singing around the campfire on those two-week campcraft trips in the Olympics. Also at Lisa's and Pat's wedding in Painted Desert years later, but not much in between.

In 2000 I bought a house in Abington, Pennsylvania, to be near Hillary and Gray and my grandchildren, Daniel and Susan. And didn't they move to Germany! Hillary had suggested I look into the Ambler Choral Society. After attending a concert, I auditioned with conductor Mark Daugherty and became one of the forty members of that prestigious group. The Ambler group performed much music that was challenging for me, and Daugherty was probably the most exacting director, but what a joyful experience.

Soon after I moved to Arizona, deafness made music impossible to appreciate or perform. My last group singing was with the small choir of what would become Sky Island Unitarian Universalist Church. I no longer sing, but my grandchildren do. Both Daniel and Susan are accomplished vocalists and violinists.

Lee

Madrigals and More

At Duke I was a Town Girl, meaning I lived at home all four years (1948-1952), except for staying on campus Freshman Week. During that week Nancy Watkins, a classmate in Brown House, suggested we try out for Madrigal Singers. "Nancy," I said, "you are out of your gourd! There are only twenty-eight singers in the Madrigal Group out of four thousand or so Duke students." But audition we did, and accepted we both were!

Eugenia Saville was a marvelous director, and the group sang lots of interesting music besides madrigals, from Gregorian chant to Benjamin Britten. Before college I sang alto – because I could. At college there were plenty of altos, so I sang soprano – because I could.

My all-time favorite teacher, Dr. Blackburn, the legendary Duke creative writing teacher, mentor of William Styron, Reynolds Price, Fred Chappell, and Anne Tyler, always came to the madrigal concerts.

At one concert I sang a set of songs by John Dowland, and Dr. Blackburn recognized me as a student in his Romantic Literature class.

Not long after that concert, Dr. Blackburn asked me if I would like to *sing* my term paper! (Are you kidding?) It seems he had long wanted to play some songs by Thomas Campion but had not been able to find recordings. So fellow student Joan Ingwerson, harpsichordist, and I put together a Thomas Campion concert. Even Dean Brinkley attended. Dr. Blackburn was so pleased he took Joan and me to the WDNC studio to make a recording of the Campion. I've been told he played that recording for his classes for years.

Lee

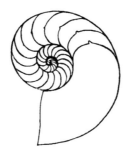

And Miles To Go

Lee

A Summer Abroad

Sailing to Europe on the Motor Ship *Nellie* was a major part of the experience. It took nine days to cross the Atlantic each way, and, yes, there was seasickness. Nearly all the passengers were college students, and in the evenings our group would gather on the fantail and sing folksongs, hymns, and golden oldies in wonderful harmony for hours. We acquired quite a following.

In the summer of 1951, I was a member of the Methodist Youth Caravan. Our group - six young men, six young women - worked in Germany and Austria shoveling World War II rubble from church sites and interacting with children and young people in youth camps. We worked and played hard; still, I gained weight from all the *Kartoffelsalat* and *Wienerschnitzel*.

After saying goodbye to our new-found friends, we twelve enjoyed a Grand Tour of Europe: Besides Germany and Austria, we toured Italy,

Lee

Switzerland, France, and England; castles, cathedrals, lakes, rivers, mountains, and glaciers.

We took the train through East Germany to Berlin past armed Russian soldiers at every station. We rode a chairlift to the top of an Alp, enjoyed a boat trip on Lake Geneva, and cruised the Rhine from Mainz to Koblenz.

In London we saw Laurence Olivier and Vivien Leigh, live, in Shakespeare's *Antony and Cleopatra* on a revolving stage. Our student tickets cost the equivalent of thirty-five cents.

In Italy I fell in love with Venice.

Fenice, Venezia, Venice

This blue and green Murano vase
recalls the sudden flights of pigeons in the Piazza,
those huge bronze horses poised atop San Marco.
Venice is a pastel place,
fading, muted,
where all is medieval mist and twilight.
Brackish water laps the barber poles
and reeks of burnt espresso,
brine, exhaust of vaporetti.
A tourist chorus sings (and echoes)
underneath damp archways.
Pale stone tracery
surrounds a space that seems to float.
The Lion of Saint Mark stands guard,
high upon his column,
and monitors the drowning of his charge.

Lee

Love, Marriage
and a Three Month Honeymoon

Herb and I met at a Gate Party.

What's a Gate Party? In 1924, when word got around that the Dukes (of Bull Durham tobacco fame and wealth) were planning to endow Trinity College, realtors bought up all the land around the small Methodist school. Shrewdly, the Trustees went out in the country and bought up hundreds of acres for the proverbial song.

The eventual result was two Duke University campuses, the older Georgian one to the east, and the newer Gothic one to the west. The road between them was considered a half-mile hyphen. Another result was a School of Forestry since the new University had all those acres of woods. Some entrances into those woods would eventually have driveways and parking areas behind locked gates, but students and friends could sign up for and get a key for a walk in the woods, a party, or a picnic.

Several of the gates had fire pits, picnic tables, and clearings for volleyball, touch football and such.

It was at one such gate party during the early days of my Senior year that I first saw Herb Lee. It was like that scene in the movie *Cyrano de Bergerac* when José Ferrer points his finger dramatically and intones, "*WHO* is that man?!" "*WHO* is *that*?" I asked Grimes, the host. Grimes was a Physics instructor and sometime date; he and I sang with the Madrigal Singers all of my four years. Grimes explained that the good-looking, dark-haired, shirtless guy playing touch football was his new roommate, back to finally finish his Senior year. I always kidded Herb that I finished Duke in the usual four years while it took him eight. He had started in the Navy V5 program, but (after washing out of flight school because of a hearing loss) he kept alternating school with work or adventure.

Grimes introduced us, and we began dating occasionally, but nothing clicked. Herb would sometimes take me to the late movies in Chapel Hill

Lee

because, as a town girl, I didn't have a curfew and the campus coeds did.

A shift came during graduation festivities. Herb had asked if I would be the week-end date for his younger brother Bill. Vea, their mother – ever protective of the younger son – asked, "Just who *is* this Pamela Cherry?" And Herb told her: "Well, she was in Modern Dance, Madrigal Singers, Student Government, Duke Players, made Dean's List, Who's Who, and Phi Beta Kappa...and he must have heard himself.

At Granny's Lake (scene of a grandmother's murder) where we all went for a picnic and swim, I was looking pretty good in my one-piece, aqua, Catalina swimsuit, but the clincher was my beating Herb in a swim race to the raft.

So we graduated. Herb headed to graduate school at Harvard and MIT, and I began work on a Master's at Columbia. When Herb wrote to ask me for a date on a Friday evening, I told my roommate he would probably ask Sue out on Saturday. Sue McMullen was a fellow Duke grad, an artist, also

100

living in NYC. But what the heck, I said; it was a date.

It turned out to be more than a date. On Friday night and most of Saturday. We petted heavily in his car on Riverside Drive, visited with his parents on Long Island, and began a semester-long commuting romance between Boston and New York.

As Herb told his roommate, Sid, "I haven't said anything to Pam, and Pam hasn't said anything to me, but both of us know that when I go down to Durham during Christmas holidays, I'll ask her to marry me, and she'll say yes." And so it was.

On March 14, 1953, we had a beautiful formal wedding in Duke University Chapel with Forest Heddon officiating. Forest was the counselor for the Methodist Youth Caravan the summer of 1951. Mary Brinkley was my Maid of Honor; childhood friend Ruthie Ledford, and Herb's sister, Carol, were bridesmaids.

As neither Herb nor I had school or work demands, we decided to travel as long as we could.

Lee

Herb and I honeymooned for three months, at Lake Junaluska, Myrtle Beach, and on both Florida coasts. Then we set out across the continent making stops wherever there were friends or National Parks to visit.

We wound up in Hawaii. But that's another story.

Bryce Canyon, 1953

After our wedding in Duke Chapel,

we took a three month honeymoon

and crossed the whole United States.

(In the process, we invented car camping.)

An April blizzard in Bryce

drove us inside the Inn for dinner,

where we met Aldyth and Ray -

on the mainland for their son's graduation -

and where we heard Aldyth say,

"Why not let them stay in your studio, dear?"

So, having a place to stay in Hawaii,

(after visiting friends in California)

we put the car and most of our belongings

in storage,

Lee

and bought two two-week round-trip tickets
to Hawaii.
(It was a Territory then.)

We stayed for two years.
And came back with a kama'aina baby
who ate her Vanda orchid lei
along the way.

Pearl Harbor, Waikiki

When we decided to stay in Hawaii, Herb easily found an engineering position at Pearl Harbor Naval Shipyard. My search for work was more frustrating: "too well-educated, too little job experience" was the refrain. Eventually someone spotted my potential, and Sylvia Wiswell took me on as a sales clerk at Liberty House Waikiki, planning to groom me to be her associate buyer to replace the one who was moving to the Mainland.

Being a fashion buyer might have been a fascinating career path, but I didn't get to follow it once I told of my pregnancy. How primitive! Nowadays women can work to full term.

(An aside: During that brief employment period I once helped Elsa Lanchester, wife to Charles Laughton, get fitted for a swimsuit.)

So, out of work, I went to the beach at Waikiki, dug a hole in the sand for my expanding belly, and worked on my tan until Lisa was born.

Lee

Hawaii High

I am walking to work, down the hill from Kaimuki,
Face to the sun, striding smartly –
Almost skipping – to an inner cadence.
My Cheshire-cat grin is almost as wide
As the pink-and-white, candy-striped skirt
Of the taffeta trousseau dress I am wearing.
We whisper together, "Shhh. Shhh".
(It's a secret.)
What a feeling!
The plain me now, for once, for sure,
Is beautiful,
Radiant, aglow, fragrant as frangipani,
And humming "Sweet Leilani".

My navy high heels keep time on the sidewalk:
Tock, tock.
(Knock, knock. Who's there?)
I am swinging a matching shoulder bag,
Carrying the child.

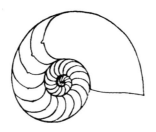

Turkey

Lee

Ak Deniz (Black Sea Cruise, 1955)

The clerk in Istanbul
*would sell us passage **to** Batum,*
*but no return. "You must book your **return***
*in **Batum**! **Those** tickets are **there**!"*
("Idiots!" he looked like to add) adding,
*"**No**! Of **course** not. No guarantees!"*

So, in an act of faith, we booked outgoing passage
with no assurance we'd get back home –
husband to Dyarbakyr, wife and babes to Ankara,
mother-in-law to Long Island.

Accommodations
were one upper and one lower bunk
*for our party of five. **You** can figure out*
out the sleeping arrangements!

Meals? I don't remember meals.
Probably I was too seasick to eat.
There was, indubitably, twice every day,

Lee

fried eggplant, "bademjahn," dripping with oil.
(Bottom john is right!)

In French, which is what people spoke
if not Turkish, "mal de mer"
doesn't sound nearly so awful as it is.
On the deck for air,
I'd have been unaware, unable to care
if my children slid into that foreign sea.
Fortunately, Nana proved a good sailor –
amused but protective.

In Trabson, or was it Samsun,
we spend a morning searching for Diogenes
searching for an honest man.

One afternoon on a black sand beach
the youngest kept eating sand.
(Some deficiency in mother's milk?)

Every time you put her down –
and she wouldn't be held –
It was hand to mouth, hand to mouth.

There was black sand in her diapers for days!

Eventually we reached Batum,
as far east as we could go. Any farther,
we'd have had to sail north and wind up in the USSR
– a big deal in those Cold War years.

As a curious footnote, twenty-five years late
– one could visit the Soviet Union by then –
I found myself in Tblisi, Georgia,
just a few kilometers east of Batum.

And, oh yes,
in Batum we were able to book our return.
And live happily ever after.

Why I Believe in UFOs

Well, for one thing it just makes sense. Think about it. How many stars are there in our own constellation, the Milky Way? How many millions, maybe billions of other galaxies are there in the known universe? How many suns in those galaxies might have orbiting planets capable of supporting life? Isn't it pretty arrogant to think that we are unique? That God or Evolution couldn't have created other Beings?

But my reasons are more particular. Even scientific. My husband, Herb, was not only brilliant, he was an electronics engineer who, in 1956, was sent on one of the most hush-hush assignments at the time. It was so hush-hush I wasn't even supposed to know what country he was in.

Of course I knew. The matter is declassified now – so I won't have to kill you if I tell you. He was in Dyarbakyr, an ancient walled city, way east in eastern Turkey, on the Tigris. He not only told me, he arranged for me and our two babies – Lisa was a year old, Hillary just eight months – to fly to Ankara where he had rented an apartment for us.

In Ankara I was pretty much on my own, as Herb could get away only for a week-end maybe once in six weeks. The landlord found some part-time help for me. Emena, who spoke not a word of English, adored my children. "Mashallah!" she would exclaim, the equivalent of "God bless." Eventually I learned a few essential words of Turkish: my address was Paris Giadessi, Yirmi-dokus. (And I can still count to ten: bir, iki, erch, dort, besh, alta, yedi, sekus, dokus, on.)

I won't go into the difficulties of trying to shop for food with my limited Turkish or having to undergo emergency gall bladder surgery in a foreign country. They aren't the point of the story.

What was at Dyarbakyr was, at the time, the world's largest radar. What was that huge radar doing? It was spying across the border to observe the Russians' attempts to send a rocket into space.

Lee

This was 1956; Sputnik was successfully launched in 1957.

The radar was not only observing, what it observed was being recorded on film twenty-four hours a day, seven days a week. Nowadays we say 24/7.

Those films of what the radar "saw" not only captured Russian early attempts to get into space. While monitoring those attempts, the films managed to capture something perhaps more significant. Strange objects would enter the filmed area at speeds unknown in that day. Maybe not even since. Not only were they faster than anything we humans had made, these objects were able to hover. It was as if they were investigating: What *are* these Earthlings up to?

You may suggest there was dust on the film, or that those sightings were caused by sunspots, or whatever. But my scientist/skeptic husband firmly believed he was witnessing evidence of other intelligent life.

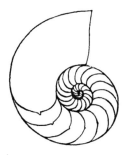

Corner to Corner

Lee

Building Houses

Herb had managed to keep that big hush-hush radar in Eastern Turkey operating 24/7. His creative fixes (though not quite paper clips, spit, and ear wax) *had* kept the radar running. Nevertheless, management decreed his make-shift repairs didn't conform to design specifications. Priorities! Herb become so disillusioned with company bureaucracy he decided to quit engineering and try his hand at building houses in Florida.

In Miami, Herb hired on as a day laborer with a licensed construction contractor who agreed to mentor him to learn the business – from the ground up, so to speak. Herb also began taking evening courses at Lindsey Hopkins in Blueprint Reading and Estimating, Dade County Code, etc. – courses he would be teaching the following year.

After a few months the contractor told Herb he had taught him all he could; Herb's next step would be to buy some property and begin building. So we

Lee

purchased two adjoining lots just west of Coral Gables. I drew floorplans for a duplex; Herb created the detailed blueprints, and we began.

We did whatever jobs we were capable of ourselves: we laid steel in the footings, juked the poured concrete. Professionals were required to pour the terrazo floors and to lay the concrete-block exterior, but Herb assisted the licensed carpenters doing the interior framing, and I painted the whole exterior. Light blue.

One day Herb came in, sweaty, dirty, and sunburned after a day nailing sheathing on the roof and announced, "I don't know when I've been so happy." Manual labor may be hard work, but it can be very satisfying.

Eventually we built two duplexes on the adjoining lots and lived in the rear half of the first one.

Our timing was poor; we had missed the Florida building boom, and Herb missed the challenges of engineering. So he returned to it.

When we came back from Turkey and could live anywhere we chose, we seriously considered Washington State but decided it was too far from the children's grandparents, all four of whom lived in the east.

Wouldn't you know! Herb's next engineering assignment was to the Naval Shipyard in Bremerton, Washington.

Hurricane Donna

The Dade County building code was designed with hurricanes in mind. It proved effective for both our duplexes in September 1960 when Donna blew in. The roofs stayed in place, and the floors stayed dry. There was just a little dampness on the towels at the windward side windows that had been intentionally left slightly open.

The Boy Scout in Herb believed in preparedness, so he had invested in an ancient second-hand diesel generator and stowed it in the garden shed he had erected. When Donna was forecast, Herb decided he'd better give Betsy a test run. No joy. So the engineer went to work. Whatever repairs he had to do took several days. When the generator finally roared to life, Herb shook his fist at the heavens as if to say, "Now do your worst!"

The heavens apparently heard him. Donna's hurricane winds blew down the huge live oak tree at the corner of our lot, and that huge tree took down the power lines with it. As our two duplexes were the only ones affected by the outage, it was a week before the repairmen got to us. That week we dined on cold meals by candlelight while Betsy noisily generated just enough electricity to keep refrigerators and freezers running in all four units, so none of us lost any food.

The down-sloping in the back yard did become a lake – maybe three feet deep at the property line. Lisa and Hillary had a wonderful time rafting on it until fire ants, desperate to not drown, came aboard and put an end to that activity. The girls got out of the water before much damage was done.

A Teacher, What Else?

When I was a child and people asked me what I wanted to be when I grew up, my answer was usually, "Anything but a teacher!" I was surrounded: Daddy was a school principal, Mother a first-grade teacher, and both of my aunts were school teachers.

Even my grandfathers had taught school: Papa Cherry before becoming a Methodist preacher/circuit rider in Western North Carolina, Granddaddy Allen in a one-room-schoolhouse to earn money for medical school.

My father clinched it for me. His follow-up to my "Anything but a teacher" was "Whatever she becomes, I hope she will be a good wife and mother." There it was, cast in stone, my future decided for me. I may have even pictured the picket fence, a rose-covered cottage, and lots of rolly-poly children.

Thus I had never aspired to a career. And I didn't have to work while Herb and I traveled –

across the continent and beyond to what was then Territory of Hawaii. Or when we lived in Turkey.

While we were building houses in Florida, Lisa was teaching herself to read. I felt she needed something more structured than I could provide, so I told Herb she needed to be in nursery school. "All right with me," he said, "but you'll have to support it."

Support it? What exactly *could* I do with no marketable skills other than a degree in English. Nevertheless, on faith I enrolled Lisa and Hillary in Country Day School and signed myself up for substitute teaching in Dade County. By November, I was thrust into full-time teaching. What else?

Thus began four years of ninety-hour work weeks for me: having to re-read the several novels I assigned but couldn't remember, lesson plans to design, tests to compose, plus the eighty to a hundred writing assignments that had to be graded every week.

Lee

What's more, I had to take evening courses at the university to earn my teaching certificate in the required three years.

Because Southwest Miami High School was in one of the largest schools districts in the country, we initiated staggered hours, and our English Department was one of the first to develop Team Teaching.

Five of the Senior English classes – over one hundred students – would meet in the little theater every day. Their five teachers would take turns being in charge, leaving the other teachers four days for preparation. My singing lecture on English Ballads and Folk Music was a winner.

To say mine was a tough schedule would be gross understatement. But I loved it. And I was good at it.

Fortunately, I had a sympathetic and supportive Department Chairman in Gretchen Hankins. Even more fortunately, Herb was a willing and capable primary parent when I was otherwise occupied.

A Tale of Two Rabbits

While we were building our first duplex, we lived in a rented house in southwest Miami, just west of Coral Gables. Lisa was probably nine, Hillary eight, when a little gray rabbit appeared on our doorstep one day. Realizing this was not some wild creature but a tame rabbit and obviously someone's pet, we asked all around the neighborhood in hopes of finding its owner. No one knew of a missing rabbit. So we adopted him. Or her.

If that bunny had a name, we've all forgotten it, but he was such a good pet. He was neat, always depositing the easy-to-clean-droppings in the same area. The girls treated that bunny like a doll, dressing him in doll's clothes, pushing him around in a doll's carriage, and cuddling him like a baby. Whether he enjoyed those ministrations or merely tolerated them, who knows?

Having missed the building boom, Herb had decided to return to engineering, and we already

Lee

had orders to move to Washington State when two young boys appeared and said, "We hear you have our rabbit." (Where had they been when we were searching for Bunny's owners!) Anyway, their timing was fortuitous.

Washington State had lots of animals to appreciate – both wild and domestic. Lisa and Hillary made the acquaintance of a man who kept a real lion in his yard. Another neighbor had several horses they could visit. Eventually they discovered a man who raised rabbits. After several of their admiring visits, the rabbit man asked Lisa and Hillary if they would like to have a rabbit. Their response being a strong affirmative, he admonished, "But you have to have your parents' permission." The girls chorused, "It's all right! It's all right! We've already had a rabbit!"

So the rabbit man disappeared briefly and returned with a rabbit he presented to the girls – a headless pink carcass, completely skinned and gutted. The girls were speechless, beyond appalled, but too polite to turn down the gift.

Once home they were free to weep and be comforted with mac and cheese for supper. Herb and I enjoyed *Hasenfeffer* later.

From One Corner to the Other

Once Herb had decided to get back into engineering, his first assignment was to the Naval Shipyard in Bremerton, Washington. He would be working on the fire-control radar on the aircraft carrier, *USS Kitty Hawk* under construction there. (As a native North Carolinian, Kitty Hawk carried special significance for me.)

So we drove diagonally across the whole continent – from the southeast corner to the northwest corner – in two Volkswagens. Herb's was a tan VW bug, mine a royal blue Karmann Ghia convertible with a white top. We traded daughters at rest stops and overnights.

As this trip happened long before the advent of cell phones, Herb devised a method for us to stay in caravan, so as to not get separated on the long trip: when the lead car wanted to change lanes, he or she would signal; the follow car would then signal and move left or right, leaving room for the lead car to slip in just in front of the follow car. It worked.

Along the way we made many memorable stops: the Badlands, the Grand Canyon, and Yellowstone where the girls enjoyed a trail ride on horseback while Herb and I got some rest. I remember stopping to eat raw asparagus right from the field in Montana's Big Sky country.

Ah! Washington State

One of the first things we did after our arrival in Washington State was look at the Kitsap County Community College catalog. I chose a course in Music Appreciation taught by Bob Dietz, a fellow Unitarian who became a good friend. I had had many hours of music at Duke such that Bob told me I ruined the curve on the exam.

Herb, who had barely seen a mountain, signed up for Advanced Mountaineering! He was in way over his head doing serious climbs with experienced Mountain Rescue guys. He stuck it out even though he would come home so exhausted he would literally have to crawl up the stairs to our second floor living quarters.

Herb was so taken with the Mountaineering, he urged me to go out for Beginning Mountaineering in the Spring. "Not me!" I said. "I like my creature comforts, and I don't like bugs." He enlisted the help of Ruth Jewel, a faculty member and climbing teacher who became a family friend; between them they persuaded me to at least give it a try.

Well, the first week-end was no challenge, just an outdoor scramble. Next was the mid-week class instruction part of the course; it was on orienting and route-finding with map and compass in preparation for the following week-end. After that experience I was sold. On one trip we climbed Cruiser and rappelled down. Our graduation climb? Mount St. Helen's before she erupted!

Summer came and I signed up for the two-week backpacking trip through Olympic National Park. The trip begins in a Temperate Rain Forest and goes through all the climate zones, Hudsonian, Alpine Meadow, even a glacier. There is an optional roped climb of Mt. Olympus, and it goes all the way to Neah Bay on the Pacific Ocean before returning to the Park entrance.

Lee

That experience was so wonderful that the following summer I wangled a staff job (as Commissary Commissar) and took Lisa and Hillary with me. Barbara Rasmussen brought her two daughters, and we made camp together. The weather was mild enough that all we needed was a tarp shelter affixed to trees with Visqueen clamps, and a ground cloth between earth and our sleeping bags.

One night, Lisa, always a rough sleeper, often fighting for her space, finally stopped disturbing us. In the morning we realized why. She and her sleeping bag had simply slid off the slippery ground cloth. We must have picked a down-sloping campsite.

A Horse for Hillary

While we lived in Florida, both Lisa and Hillary took riding lessons. Both girls enjoyed riding, but horses became a passion for Hillary. Not long after we moved to Washington State, Herb suggested we get her a horse for her birthday. "A horse! Nobody in my family ever had a horse!" I exclaimed. But everywhere we looked there were horses.

Fred Clarke, a neighbor, just happened to be the county Four-H Club adviser. What a character! Fred was a grizzled old guy, built like a fireplug who had won all sorts of prizes in rodeos. With his champion horse, Jadah, Fred could rope a steer without his hands on the reins.

Naturally we enlisted Fred's help in selecting a horse for Hillary. We looked at several horses that Fred deemed would be suitable for a young rider. On one occasion we visited a blue-eyed, black and white, part Morgan (full-size body, short legs). As we

Lee

left, Hillary asked, "Are we going to look at any more horses before we get Archie?"

Thus Archie became part of the family. He lived just down the street with Jadah and Fred, but, under Fred's tutelage, Hillary was responsible for Archie's feeding, watering, and grooming. She rode that horse bareback all over town, sometimes with Lisa or a friend aboard. It was a wonderful companionship.

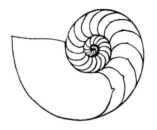

Because It Is There

Lee

Learning to Climb

We have practiced ice-ax arrest,

and how to glissade safely;

we have spent a night in the snow cave

we dug and shaped with spoons and cups.

In crevasse-rescue exercise,

we climbed dark echoic walls of ice

with sling ropes Prussik'd on the climbing rope,

connecting bowline on the waist to belay above.

An act of faith.

Layered in sun-screen and long sleeves,

we have baked and broiled in fearsome heat

and glacier glare.

We have been so cold in overnight bivouacs

we feared for fingers and toes,

Lee

watching the condensation from our breath

freeze against the inside of the tent.

Those aching backs, heavy packs,

sore leg muscles, well-worn moleskin,

bruised, black toenails, and

end-of-day "sewing-machine" knees

do earn rewards:

After a long, pre-dawn climb

to surface above a sea of clouds at sunrise.

Mount Ranier

It took me three attempts to climb Mount Ranier.

At 14,400 feet, Mount Ranier is the highest of the volcanic peaks of the Cascades. The mountain, also called Tacoma or Tahoma, last erupted in 1894; it is still considered active but is presently dormant.

On the first attempt I was the only woman on a two-day climb with half a dozen Mountain Rescue guys who intended an assault by a route different from the customary one via Paradise Glacier.

I knew I needed to travel light, so instead of porting a tent for the overnight, I constructed a shell of rip-stop nylon only slightly larger than my sleeping bag and Ensolite ground cover. It was perfect.

After we set up camp and had supper, I went looking for some privacy for a bathroom break and

Lee
figured the huge rock pile below our campsite was pretty much out of the guys' line of sight. To steady myself while lowering all my layers, I placed my hand on a boulder only to have it roll over my left little finger before cascading in a small avalanche down the mountain. Needless to say, I was shaken. The evidence of a broken first joint is still with me.

Three o'clock next morning we roped up, me between two of the men, and began to ascend single file. The route was extremely icy, and my hand hurt when I had to use my ice axe on the left.

About daybreak we aborted, the leader having determined the conditions were just too dangerous.

My second attempt was with husband Herb and Fred Smith, a colleague of Herb's at work in the Bremerton Shipyard. The three of us were taking the conventional route, intending to overnight in the hut above Paradise Glacier. The day was gorgeous, and we could easily have made the summit had there not been about three feet of new snow. Breaking trail was tortuous, and our progress was so slow that

Herb realized we would run out of time if we continued. We were disappointed, but we knew it was the right decision.

I would never have made the summit on the third try if two friends hadn't practically dragged me up the final pitch. The summit isn't really a peak; instead there's a caldera, a bowl-shaped crater formed by a major eruption leading to the collapse of the mouth of the volcano. The caldera was full of snow and, thankfully, quiet and peaceful.

Our house on Sylvan Way was on the highest elevation in Bremerton. From the picture window in our living room we could watch the ferries plying Puget Sound and, on a clear day, Mount Ranier.

From the crest of that hill we could see the whole Olympic Range. By the time we left Washington State in 1967, we had climbed most of the higher Olympic mountains. And with groups like the Seattle Mountaineers I had climbed a number of the volcanic peaks in the Cascades: Mount Baker,

Lee

Mount Hood, Mount Shasta, Mount Ranier (the highest at 14,411 feet), and Mount St. Helen's.

Mount St. Helen's was our graduation climb for the Beginning Mountaineering Course at Kitsap Community College, which, if I'm not mistaken, was the first accredited mountaineering course in the country. When I climbed her, Mount St. Helen's was a perfectly symmetrical cone. She erupted spectacularly in 1980.

Apple Nut Bread

Whenever we went climbing
In Olympics or Cascades,
We always hoped John Butler would be there.
John was an accomplished climber as a teen,
And he always brought with him several
Loaves of his mother's scrumptious,
Soggy, apple nut bread –
Enough to share.

I still have the recipe.
But where...?

John, still only in his twenties,
John Butler got blown away in a blizzard
On Denali.

Lee

Base Camp Above the Blue Glacier

Kitsap Community College in Washington State sponsored numerous backpacking and mountain-climbing trips during our stay in Bremerton. One such was a ten-day Advanced Mountaineering trip with the intent of climbing some hitherto unclimbed peaks in the Olympics.

Husband Herb and I were among that party. Base camp was to be above the Blue Glacier in Olympic National Park. To reach the Blue Glacier, one goes through all the climate zones. The route transits a temperate rainforest, follows the scenic Hoh River Trail, and crosses an alpine meadow to reach the lateral moraine at the foot of the dramatically flowing glacier.

The Blue Glacier is marked by crevasses and bergschrunds, and crossing it requires experience as well as special equipment such as crampons and ice axes in addition to climbing ropes. (We also carried smaller Prusik ropes in case we had to climb out of a crevasse.)

On such long trips, mules carried our food and other supplies as far as they could. It was up to the climbers to ferry what we would need across the glacier. That project necessitated several crossings. The first was to deposit the contents of our expedition backpacks at base camp. The second was a crossing to ferry supplies. On one crossing my pack weighed seventy-five pounds.

Late in the afternoon we got settled at a wonderful, reasonably level campsite overlooking the glacier where we set up our tents and cooking stoves and made supper. It had been a beautiful day, but the weather turned about the time we turned in. It rained, and it rained, and it rained. All night. Calls of nature were excruciating as it was just above freezing outside as well as wet. Conditions weren't much better in our tents where the water ran inside and thoroughly soaked us and our sleeping bags. It was definitely one of the most miserable nights I ever tried to sleep through.

Lee

By morning the rain had stopped and the sun, brilliant at altitude, came blazing forth. After we changed into whatever dry clothing survived, we strung lines between tent poles for hanging our dripping down sleeping bags. Amazingly, they were dry by evening.

Several members of the group, including Herb, did make some first ascents. Not I. I was content to do lesser climbs and excursions. Still, it was a memorable trip.

A Try for Whitney

(Mount Whitney, in the Sierra Nevada, is the highest summit in the contiguous United States with an elevation of 14,505 feet. -Wikipedia)

Whenever someone says, "I tried," the implication is that he or she didn't succeed. That was certainly true of our party of six when we made an attempt to climb Whitney.

Although Whitney is the highest mountain in the United States outside of Alaska, the eleven-mile Mount Whitney Trail Route is considered a class 1 climb, or a walk-up. I reckoned that for my daughters it would be a breeze. After all, they had already climbed Mount Olympus. Though only slightly above 9,000 feet, Olympus is considered one of the "Five Majors." It involves a 17-mile approach, a roped crossing of the Blue Glacier with its crevasses and bergschrunds, and a Class 4 rock climb (with a 5th Class step) on loose rocky ramps to the summit.

Lee

Six of us started out to conquer Whitney, two adults and four pre-teen girls: Fred Smith, a colleague of Herb's with his two Rasmussen step-daughters, Lisa, Hillary, and me. To make it easier for the girls, Fred and I each carried a tent, a ground cloth, a stove, and food and water in our expedition packs. The four girls' rucksacks had to carry only their sleeping bags, a jacket for when it got colder, water, and trail snacks.

We made camp, set up the tents and had supper before dark. Lisa, unfortunately, was suffering from altitude sickness at around 12,000 feet, and the Rasmussen girls were complaining of fatigue and sore muscles.

Consequently, in the early morning of the gorgeous next day, Fred and his daughters bailed and headed home. Hillary and I left Lisa to sleep in the tent while we two made for the summit. True to the printed information, the trail was easy, just a slow snow slog one could almost have done in sneakers.

About mid-morning the weather changed, and Hillary and I found ourselves in white-out conditions. As with Etna, still to come, we aborted. Without my altimeter, we had no idea whether we were one hundred or fifteen hundred feet from the summit.

Maybe you can argue about politics or religion, but you can't argue with the weather.

In Search of the Oldest Living Thing

In the late 1960's, when we made our excursion to see them, Bristlecone Pines were believed to be the world's oldest living things. That is, if you don't count bacteria which go back in fossil records to 3.5 billion years.

(from Wikipedia: *One of the three species of pines, Pinus longaeva, is among the longest-lived life forms on Earth. The oldest Pinus longaeva is more than 5,000 years old, making it the oldest known individual of any species;*

The Ancient Bristlecone Pine Forest is a protected area high in the White Mountains in Inyo County in eastern California. The Great Basin Bristlecone Pine (Pinus longaeva) trees grow between 9,800 and 11,000 feet above sea level, in xeric alpine conditions, protected within the Inyo National Forest.

The Methuselah Grove in the Ancient Bristlecone Pine Forest is the location of the

"Methuselah," a Great Basin Bristlecone Pine that is 4,848 years old. For many years, it was the world's oldest known living non-clonal organism, until superseded by the discovery in 2013 of another bristlecone pine in the same area with an age of 5,066 years (germination in 3051 BC). "Methuselah" is not marked in the forest, to ensure added protection from vandals.)

This grove we needed to see. (We lived briefly in southern California after leaving Washington and before heading for Italy.) So one day, while Herb was at work, I packed my daughters and a picnic lunch in the Karmann Ghia convertible, and we set out for the White Mountains to see these Bristlecone Pines. The poor air-breathing vehicle struggled with the altitude, but we made it.

Imagine the feeling of looking at a living tree that began life three thousand years before the Christian era. Still more amazing is that these ancient trees thrive in the most difficult of conditions: an extremely dry, rocky environment at altitude. In fact they resist transplanting to more favorable conditions.

These trees are "non-clonal," but as it happens, the oldest presently known living organism is clonal, the lowly creosote bush, and it is located nearby. Had we but known.

King Clone, in the Mojave Desert, is thought to be the oldest creosote bush ring. Unobtrusive it may be, but this bush ring is estimated to be 11,700 years old. It is probably the oldest living organism on Earth, centuries older than the redwoods or the Bristlecone Pines.

Mount Olympus and Mount Olympos

While we lived in Washington State, our nuclear family, Lisa, Hillary, Herb and I, all managed to climb Mount Olympus at least once. Olympus can't compare in elevation with the volcanic peaks of the Cascades, but it is considerably harder to get to and is a challenging ascent usually involving roping up with a more experienced climber.

Olympus is just under 8,000 feet, but since a climb starts at close to sea level, one gains almost that much in altitude. Despite its relatively low elevation, Olympus supports five glaciers, and one must cross the Blue Glacier to climb it. The Blue Glacier is one of the most studied glaciers on the planet, primarily because it is one of the lowest lying glaciers anywhere. Caltech does research there most summers. We have been inside one of their ice caves.

Before we left Italy in 1972, Herb and I took the train north to Stuttgart to pick up a 280 SL

Lee

Mercedes he had ordered – one of those mid-life guy things. (Later I got to drive it over 100 miles per hour on a straight stretch of Italian autostrada.) From Germany, Herb drove the two of us south to Greece. We crossed the Alps through Austria, thence into what we then called Jugoslavia, now divided into several countries.

We passed through Zagreb; we stopped to admire the beautiful and famous three-arched Latin Bridge in Sarajevo where Archduke Ferdinand was assassinated in 1914, an event that led to the First World War. We swam in the Adriatic from a pebbled beach not far from Dubrovnik. Dubrovnik is a handsome walled city, one I would later revisit with my grandchildren who were on tour in the Balkans with their chamber orchestra.

In Macedonia, Herb and I spent two nights in Litochoro in order to climb the other Mount Olympos. The one in Greece requires climbers to be accompanied by an official guide. Our company included an elderly ex-ski-trooper from Germany,

Herb and me, the very young Greek guide, and his still younger German Shepard.

The puppy had obviously made the ascent with the guide many times and was fearless. I, on the other hand, was spooked by the exposure on a narrow, rocky ledge and asked for a rope. So the adults roped up – except for the macho German who disdained such aid.

One of the rules we learned in mountaineering classes was always to descend by the route you ascended unless that route was deemed unsafe or impossible. Imagine our surprise when, after a break at the summit, the guide headed across the top and down the back side.

The guide was bounding ahead, moving fast "heeling down" on a long, wide snow field. Herb and I looked at each other wondering "Why isn't he glissading? You can see a clear, level run-out." We had our ice axes to use as rudders; Herb's climbing pants had a faux leather seat, so he sat in the snow, I straddled him, and we began a glorious glissade down the back side of Olympos.

Lee

At least it was fun until the Shepard bounded back and began to bite our clothing to try to slow our descent. Then the fun became funny. Clearly that puppy believed we were in trouble and tried valiantly to save us.

Cuckoo

At home, cozy on the couch,
on a cold and rainy afternoon,
across the water from Seattle,
I hear Respighi's The Birds on radio KRAB,
and experience time-warp....

Herb and I are once more
back where we left the car,
hot, dry, dusty, and beyond tired
after a two-day climb of (our second) Mount Olympos
(The first was here, in Washington State.)

Life becomes somewhat restored
with the aid of the too-warm lemonade
we drink, standing by the car near Litochoro,
our day
made magical by
(Did you hear that!)
a mere two notes of bird song.

Lee

*Pamela's great-great grandmother Dorcas Tomlinson Turner
(1813 – 1900)*

158

Allen great-grandparents, Faitha Elizabeth Wooten and William Marion Allen

Cherry grandparents, Julia Allen Hix & William Samuel Cherry

Allen grandparents, Pamela Wyche & Joseph Augustus Allen

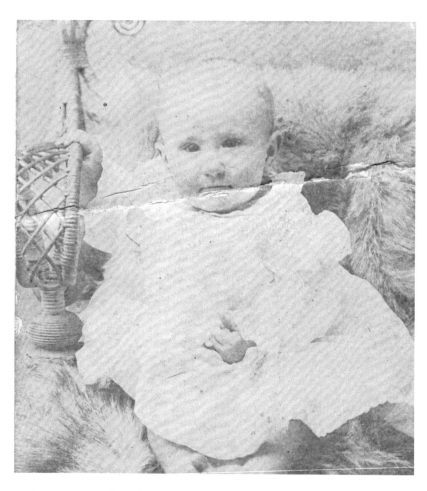

Pamela's father, baby William Hix Cherry (1897 – 1971)

Pamela's mother, baby Julia Wyche Allen (1904 – 1994)

Julia Wyche and Hix Cherry,
wedding picture December 31, 1924

Hix Cherry, Pamela, age 3, Julia Wyche Cherry

Pamela peeking from teacherage porch, Bahama, N.C.

Four generations, 1930: Great-grandfather Allen Hambeth Hix; Grandmother Julia Allen Hix Cherry; Father Hix Cherry; baby Julia Pamela

Grandaddy & Mima Allen, Pamela & baby William (Bill), 1935

Pamela & Bill, 1941

Hix & Julia Wyche Cherry

The family, 1948: Hix, Pamela, & Julia Wyche Cherry, Arthur Garceau, Bill Cherry, Blackie, & Shin Tanaka

Headed for New England, 1948; Ruth Ledford, Bill, Julia Wyche, Pamela, and Hix Cherry

Granddaddy and Mima Allen, and Great Aunt Florence

*Bill Cherry &
Blackie the dog*

*Mephistopheles
(Fisty) the cat*

Daddy with his mackerel

Durham High senior play Pride and Prejudice, *1948; Pamela* (Elizabeth), *Jimmy Heldman* (D'arcy)

Maria *(Pamela Cherry) scolds* Sir Toby Belch *(Bob Grahl) in Duke Players production of* Twelfth Night

SING 250-YEAR-OLD MUSIC —
Duke University Madrigal Singers Arthur O'Steen and Pamela
Cherry of Durham (center) look
over the score of a musical son-
net written 250 years ago, Miss

Cherry and Joan Ingw
Middletown, O., (right) h
completed recordings of
of Elizabethan sonnets
and set to music by
Campion. The Duke g

Duke University Madri
Search Out the Lost T

By MARGARET PULLIG
DURHAM, May 31. — What kind
of guest would you be at a dinner

rhythm with the four or
"melodies" being sung a
time.

*Duke Madrigal
Singers, 1951;
Arthur O'Steen,
Pamela Cherry,
Joan Ingwersen*

*Pamela,
Modern Dancer,
1952*

173

Pamela on the Left Bank, Paris, 1951

Duke Chapel Wedding, March 14, 1953

Herb & Pamela checking out a wedding gift, 1953

The honeymooners, Myrtle Beach, S.C.

Pearl Harbor, Territory of Hawaii

On the beach at Waikiki, 1953

Four generations, 1954; Julia Wyche and Hix Cherry, Joseph and Pamela Allen, Herb and Pamela Lee with Baby Pamela Elisabeth Lee (Lisa)

*Motherhood:
Pamela with
Lisa and Baby
Hillary Susan*

Young Lisa & Hillary

179

Hillary & Archie, 1965

Pamela & Herb, rest stop after a climb, Washington State

Bill with sons Bob and Charles in 1965, with Corky the dog in Pamela's Karmann Ghia

Lee

Four siblings: Hix Cherry, Mabel Cherry, Estelle Cherry Lawing, Hugh Cherry

Ms. Lee,
English teacher,
1960

HERB LEE (right) takes a compass reading as he and other Sub
Aqua Club members, (r. to l.) Dusty Blades, Pam Lee, Dick
Gilchrist and Les Whitney, prepare to dive into the sea near
Gaeta.

Diving near Gaeta,
Italy, 1971

Skiing
at Rocarasso,
Italy, 1970

Pamela at Machu Picchu, 1979, en route to Argentina

Herb & Pam sharing a yerba mate at Quinta "El Conejito,"
Argentina, 1980

The "kerosene man"
(see poems Winter & Verano *in section* "Argentina")

Lee

Turner Family Reunion, 1987; Susan Baldwin, Bill Cherry, Julia Wyche Cherry, Pamela Lee

*Lisa Lee and Pat
Sullivan; Painted
Desert, April 1, 1989*

*Harold (Jake)
Jacobsen,
Louise
Decker,
Hillary Lee
and Gray
Safford,
at the Decker
Estate, July
14, 1990*

187

"The Lady Equitable" 5k run, 1981, Suzan Dentry, Pamela Lee, Cora Dentry

Pamela finishes New York Marathon, 1991

Bill & Pamela, 1991

Four generations, 1992: Grandmother Pamela, Great-grandmother Julia Wyche, mother Hillary Lee, and baby Daniel Lee Safford

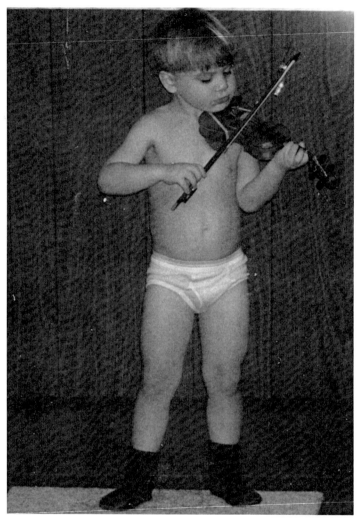

Daniel Safford and tiny violin

Susan Safford's first violin recital

Daniel kisses little sister Susan

The Lees at Gettysburg (with Gokenbachs and Saffords)

Pamela walked up Mt. Sinai, Israel, rode down, 1997

Near the Parthenon, Athens on Greece tour with Bill, 1997

Guru Swami-gal from Kerala (see "Epiphany")

Susan Baldwin at the Ramana Ashram

Tea harvesting above the clouds, Darjeeling, India, 1999

U Taam, Pam's sherpa on the Everest, turning giant prayer wheel, Nepal, 1999

Two Buddhist nuns after Muktinath, Nepal, 1999

Reflections

Three generation 5k run, Abington, Pennsylvania, Hillary, Pamela, Susan & Daniel

Daniel & Susan helping with Pamela's garden, Turner Avenue, Abington, Pennsylvania

Proud Grandmother Pamela with Susan and Daniel, violinists

Daniel, Susan, Pamela by the Rhine, Düsseldorf, Germany, 2003

Daniel & Susan play for Aunt Estelle at friends homes

Daniel Safford as Jean Valjean in Les Miserables,
Abington High School, 2010

Susan Safford, 2015, senior recital, Susquehanna University

Lee

Aunt Estelle
(lived to age 106)
at her 100th
birthday party

Herb resists hugs from daughters Hillary and Lisa

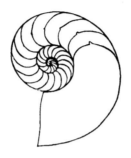

Italy

Lee

Vintage Villa Coppola

To get to Villa Coppola from Napoli, take the coast road past Bagnoli, and, before you reach Pozzuoli (once a key port of Imperial Rome), turn right at Terme Puteole (a Roman bath mentioned by Paul in *Acts*), climb the dirt track four switchbacks, and you're there.

Or, you could walk down the hundred fifty steps from a bus stop on Via Domiziana, the main road north from Naples to Rome.

The Villa Coppola compound is (as most are) formidably fenced. And where the fuchsia bougainvillea cascades over the gate, you must push a buzzer (or use your key) to gain admittance.

When you enter the flagstone patio, go straight, and you will pass a tree-sized lantana outside the kitchen. (The kitchen has a real marble countertop.) Then climb up outside stairs to the rooftop deck with a Mediterranean view to "See Naples and die" for.

Lee

To approach the front door, turn right as you enter the gate. Inside, the whole interior is floored with dark green tile with occasional white floral tiles for accent. (Extra tiles we used for trivets. Still do.) Off the dining-living room is a sort of den or small office with a seldom-used telephone and a *well*-used Hermes manual typewriter.

Twin lamps, made of amphorae that Herb found diving, grace the living space. (The NATO archaeologist identified them as BCE.) This salon and the larger bedrooms all have French doors which open onto a balcony that runs the whole length of the villa, same view as the upper deck.

Another set of stairs, this one festooned with fragrant jasmine, descends from balcony to a garden where rosebushes line the fences, and a ceramic dwarf, a "nano," serves as guardian spirit.

There *was* one thorn in Paradise. See, this was a summer villa, a place where *Famiglia Coppola* could escape the city heat, an abode not intended for wintering. And winter we did. For five years. Though mild, compared with New England or

Minnesota, southern Italy can be cold. (I've seen snow on Vesuvius.) And our kerosene heaters just weren't up to the task.

To keep warm, Herb went to work, the girls to school. At home I snuggled under the covers and read books with mittens on my hands – not easy turning pages – and thawed out on week-end ski trips to the Abruzzi.

But back to the garden: down yet more stairs, one reached a lower terrace with fruit trees, and where vegetables grew inside hip-high hedges of rosemary. That's where the serious grape arbor was.

Each year we'd ask the landlord's gardener - in our fractured, halting *Napolitán* - "Could we make some wine from our grapes?" And every year he'd tell us not to bother – he'd give us some of his. (A generous gesture, but we had enjoyed better wine.)

Our last year there, the new gardener asked "Why don't you make some wine from your grapes?" He didn't understand our laughter. But he kindly took us through the process: when to harvest, how long to leave the grapes in the sun, where to buy a chestnut cask which would swell to watertight when soaked.

(Just try to find a chestnut-wood vat in the States now! Although, I've heard that **before** the blight, an enterprising squirrel could have run chestnut to chestnut from Maine to Georgia without touching ground.)

Anyway, on an auspicious day, (having previously washed our feet) Hillary and I lifted our skirts, stepped into the vat, and trod on unwashed grapes.

After some days the juice began to whisper. Daily, Aurelio would taste and say, "Not yet," and scientist Herb would check with saccharimeter. Eventually we skimmed and strained and bottled the purple brew in slim green bottles. It was a harsh, uncompromising red, but it was ours: Vintage Villa Coppola, 1972.

Ambrosia

George Martin,

almost eighty, and fresh from climbing

in the Alps (and his second Mount Olympus)

came to visit us in Naples – Pozzuoli, actually.

Doubtless we toured the "Campi Flegri,"

(our "Flaming Fields"

whose Terme Puteole Paul pays tribute to in Acts),

the furmaroles of Sulfatara, our local volcano,

an overnight mountain,

and signs of slow-moving earthquakes

in the so-called Temple of Serapis.

We looked at the entrance to Hades at Lago D'Averno,

mused in the amphitheater on the Domiziana,

and sought the Cumaean Sybil

just up the road near Arco Felice.

Lee

And after all,

what became the indelible memory

began with a late afternoon visit

to the "Temple of Apollo" –

not a temple, really,

but the eroded half-dome of a ruined Roman Bath –

where local "agricolae" offered us

potatoes they were harvesting.

Our meal that evening –

principally those new potatoes

freshly dug from the Temple of Apollo –

savored as we watched the winking lights

of night-fishermen off Capo Miseno –

seemed food for gods,

the three of us harmonious and wise.

European Grand Tour

In the summer of 1969, not long after our arrival in Italy, my two daughters and I made a circuit of the Continent in a tan Volkswagen Beetle: Italy, San Moreno, Austria, Switzerland, Germany, East Germany, Belgium, France, Monaco and back to Italy. (Spain and England would come later.)

It was my objective to visit as many of the major art museums in Europe as possible. Mission accomplished:

In Venice we were awed by Michelangelo's David at the Academia and by the modern art collection in Peggy Guggenheim's palazzo on the Grand Canal. We saw the remarkable stamp collection in San Moreno, paintings by Durer and Velasquez in Vienna's Kunsthistoriches Museum.

In Germany we walked through Checkpoint Charlie to get to the Dahlem Museum in East Berlin in order to see the bust of Nefertiti.

Lee

There were Rembrandts and Van Goghs in Amsterdam, Breugels in Brussels. And in Paris we were impressed by the Impressionists at the Jeu de Paume in the Tuileries Gardens. (The Impressionists now reside in the Musee D'Orsay.) At the Louvre we gazed at Venus de Milo and the Mona Lisa.

Back in Italy we were in Milan long enough to visit Leonardo's fresco of *The Last Supper*. Thence to Florence and the world-famous housing my favorite Botticellis. The Leaning Tower of Pisa does look precarious. Did Galileo really experiment there?

In Rome we did the obligatory tour of the Colosseum, the Forum, the Trevi Fountain, the Spanish Steps. We walked in St. Peter's Square and stood in awe beneath the Ceiling of Michelangelo's Sistine Chapel.

My teenage daughters may have felt that trip a drag at times, but as adults they are appreciative of and grateful for the experience.

When we set out from Naples, we had a detailed itinerary but not a single hotel or hostel reservation, yet the only time we failed to find a place to stay was upon arriving at Mont Saint Michel in Normandy on the first day of the British *and* the French annual holiday. There wasn't a room to be had within fifty kilometers. I leave you to imagine the configuration of three full-size females spending the night in a VW bug.

Our reward? We awoke to watch the morning tide run in over the mudflats and levitate that ethereal island.

Night Dive Near Napoli

Herb was away on a sea trial, so I went in his place on a night dive with his diving buddy Shumow. Eight of us, wearing wet suits, masks, snorkels and fins, enter the water from the Baia shore. We surface swim (saving air) to deeper water, and two by two submerge. The others soon are only distant glow. I follow close behind my buddy Shumow.

Our lights illumine sea life seldom seen by day: sea cucumbers, eels, *et cetera*. Shu angles down, negotiates a narrow space between rock faces, and peers into a cave. He gestures me to look. I look – the other way. Finally I shake my head, "Not me!" (I'm fearful of hanging a tank.) Again Shu taps his mask and points insistently. He won't give up. So I swim down, peer into the cave, and, all indignant, shrug, "What?" Shu points again. I peer again and realize I'm seeing eyes! Two eyes. Two feet apart! A smiling mouth. Whoa!

Nothing to fear: this giant grouper, grown too large to leave his cave, waits there for dinner to appear.

Shu spots a friendly squid and stows him in the catch net on his belt. Oops! Squid *and* net escape. Shu captures both, hands me the squid to hold while he secures the net. Tentacles and suckers gently squeeze my arm. Then squid turns off my light! But Shu shines his and four arms wrestle eight arms back in sack. The squid escapes again, looks back, awaiting our pursuit: "Tag! You're it!" he seems to say. We chase. Squid teases, pauses, flees.

I laughed so hard I nearly lose my mouthpiece. In any case, we're out of air, so surface under stars and snorkel all the long way home. (We were really out to sea!) We waded in mere moments before our worried friends (who'd reached the beach a good half hour before) would have called the Shore Patrol.

High Drama

Medea was playing
in the ancient amphitheater in Pompei.

Elinor, the girls' Latin teacher,
came with us.

On that memorable evening,
we watched two dramas unfold:

The Greek tragedy on stage,
and – as a backdrop – a total lunar eclipse.

Salad Days

In salad days – our gathering and **not**-spending
days – we visited Malta's Dingli Cliffs.
There was the long, hot, sticky climb in the sun
to reach the top overlooking the sea, then
overlooking each other, no longer aware
of the sun or the sea,
waves washing over us, wet skin glowing,
vapor rising in the breathless air,
joined in the then and there, where, later –
surprised to discover thyme on our hands –
we lingered to garner dusty, fine leaves.

Wild thyme. Wild thyme.
Now there is a smell
(however essence and pungency pass)
I can summon without benefit (or beneficence)
of dry leaves in glass.

Lee

In that time of loving
we lay on lines
along rippled cart-track ridges,
radiant prehistoric grooves
inscribed in rock –
lines that had served as purpose for our visit.
Those ridges that had pressed into our backs
were etched into that limestone centuries before.

Were they authentic Paleolithic travois tracks
converging to a market place?
Or merely erosion patterns
recording where years of rainwater ran?

I'd rather believe
remote ancestors gathered there,
exchanged their goods and gossip –
garnered some thyme –
And, like us, lingered for love.

Sicily

While we were living in Italy, Herb's mother came to visit us in Pozzuoli, a suburb of Naples. When the girls had their Spring Break from Forest Sherman High School, the four of us set out to tour Sicily. It was just the four females; Herb was off somewhere – to Spain, Malta, or on sea trials.

As I was the only one of us with a European driver's license, I did all the driving. Our vehicle was that same tan VW bug in which Lisa, Hillary, and I once spent the night when there was no lodging to be had anywhere near Mont Saint-Michel.

We headed south from Naples, drove past Vesuvius and Pompei, around the Amalfi coast, and all the way to the toe of the Italy boot at Reggio, Calabria. We could have taken a ferry from Naples to Palermo, but there was much of southern Italy to see by going overland, and, by driving, we would have transportation while in Sicily.

Lee

From Reggio it was a short ferry ride across the narrow Strait of Messina, linking the Tyrrhenian Sea to the north and the Ionian Sea to the south. The strait has been known since antiquity for its treacherous waters.

In Homer's *Odyssey*, Circe warns Odysseus about the two monsters, Scylla (the rock) and Charybdis (the whirlpool), who made passage through the strait a challenge, if not a disaster, for mariners. Our passage was uneventful.

From Messina we went west along the northern coast to Palermo, Sicily's capitol and its most populous city. If we saw any Mafiosos there, we were unaware.

After rounding the western tip of the island, our route ran southeast. One afternoon we stopped for lunch in a small restaurant overlooking the sea where I enjoyed possibly the best shrimp ever, and Lisa said much the same about her fungi or mushrooms.

Our destination on the southwestern coast was Agrigento and its Valley of Temples where some of the best Greek temples from the 5th Century BCE have survived. It was springtime, and the almond trees were in blossom.

Scenic beauty abounded as we continued our circumnavigation. Having reached the southeast promontory, our route next took us north to Siracusa, or Syracuse, where there is a well-preserved 5th Century BCE amphitheater. Its seats were carved out of the rock, and it faces Mount Etna, Europe's highest volcano.

Further north, the town of Taormina is handsomely situated on a 700-foot elevation overlooking the sea on one side and Mount Etna on the other. Like Siracusa, Taormina boasts an ancient Greek amphitheater.

But before we reached Taormina, there was Catania, and from Catania one can climb Mount Etna. We four females took a cable car to the Etna Observatory where Lisa decided to stay with her

Lee

grandmother while Hillary and I set out to try for the summit.

Mount Etna, an 11,000-foot cone, is an active volcano, one that has been active since ancient times. It still has eruptions, the most recent occurring in 2015-2016. There are videos of that spectacular event.

Etna is not a difficult climb. It's just a regular snow slog, and not especially steep. Nevertheless, Hillary and I did not make the summit. After an hour or so we ran into white-out conditions and turned back, having no idea whether we were 1,000 feet or 10 feet from the top.

Backpacking in Crete

Joy Ballinger and I met on a two-week backpacking/climbing trip sponsored by Kitsap Community College in Bremerton, Washington. Joy really took to mountaineering and became an excellent and experienced climber. She was already a world traveler, having gone as an adjunct teacher or as the wife of the tour leader with University of Oregon travels abroad.

I was living in Italy in 1969 when Joy suggested I meet her in Athens to tour Crete. I was already in love with Minoan culture and architecture, having read the Mary Renault novels, so I said, "Yes!" (The Minoan civilization, 2700 - 1420 B.C. is the oldest known European civilization.) After a few days in Athens we took the overnight ferry to Heraklion where beautiful snow-capped mountains greeted our arrival.

We toured the ancient historic sites of Knossos and Phaestos early on. Before too long we managed to connect with the Crete Climbing Club and arranged to accompany them on a climb of Mount Ida, the supposed birthplace of Zeus. We did not reach the summit, as Joy got desperately ill about halfway – probably a combination of food poisoning and altitude sickness. Thanks to the ministrations of fellow climber and nurse, Evangelina Koutsabou, Joy recovered, but it was scary.

Once away from the big cities Heraklion and Chania we were quite the curiosity: two older women in shorts and climbing boots, carrying huge expedition backpacks. We probably shocked or titillated the Greek men in their baggy pants, smoking or drinking Turkish coffee outside the tavernas, but were greeted warmly by the rural black-garbed women who would bring us tea or rose petal jam when we passed their dooryards. Always they greeted us with a friendly *Kali mera!* or *Kali spera!* (Good morning or Good afternoon.)

What did we eat? With little or no Greek, mostly we would look at whatever dishes were on display in tavernas or small shops and point to whatever looked appetizing. A favorite was the thick Greek yogurt. We consumed a lot of halvah, a soft, fudge-like candy made from tahini or sesame paste.

Our main objective was to hike the Samaria Gorge, reputedly the latest gorge in Europe. Guidebooks had assured us it could be done in one day, so we left early to get a bus to the trail head. The guidebooks were wrong. We endured innumerable crossings of the icy stream that bisected the island north to south, sometimes carrying our boots and socks to keep them dry.

As it began to get dark, we realized we would have to spend the night on the trail. Thank goodness for the lightweight space blanket I always carried in my pack. It served as ground cloth and cover for the two of us.

In the morning we met a woman gathering dandelion greens near Sfakia on the southern coast (Lybian Sea) where we arrived too late to catch the daily mail boat – only to learn that a couple of Germans had commandeered the only hotel room in town. The hotel folks did find a loft for Joy and me to

Lee

sleep in. Of course we had our sleeping bags and Ensolite, but it was a restless night as there was no way to secure the access to the loft, and noises (of wind? Or of rats?) kept us awake. That night was the only night I ever kept my pocket knife open by my side though there turned out to be no need of it.

That morning we took the mail boat back to civilization – accompanied by a shepherd carrying a sheep across his shoulders, looking remarkably like the archaic statue in the Athens museum.

Tell Me, Daedalus

Did you take pride

in pacifying Pasiphae, then mollifying Minos

with ingenious plans to hide

the monstrous get of his wife's unseemly passion –

Poseidon and her ardor satisfied – inside

designs conceived of in the labyrinthine windings of

your mind?

How came you to side

with the love-struck daughter? To confide in her

who would provide her captive captivating lover

thread to wind up all your ingenious ways,

and emerge triumphant from the maze,

the girl a trophy at his side?

Were you so preoccupied

(with past success or future fame)

Lee

it made you blind to the wrath of that father

(half out of his mind with grief and rage)

who would have you consigned to,

cast inside the very convolutions

you so cunningly designed?

Or did you simply decide to stay

without wondering why,

realizing that – whether or not confined

and bored out of mind – you still would have tried

those damned wings,

contrived to manufacture things

of candle-wax and pigeon moult, because the sky

is there! And man must fly!

Artistic urgings aside, Daedalus,

how could you bide the anguish?

Was your creative fire forever quenched

in that fell moment, watching waters divide?

Have you grieved, Daedalus,

an Abraham unreprieved?

Steadfastly cried

it was enough that one of you believed?

Do you lie open-eyed

at night, debating whether it were wrong or right

to fledge the boy and set him free,

to wish him joy in his brief flight

only to see him fall headlong into the sea?

Did something of you die with his wild cry

and plunge into that unforgiving tide?

Or were you satisfied,

in general, with the experiment,

gravity and parenthood at once denied?

Then – earth and sky being free – were you content

to shrug once, and proceed to Sicily? Whence,

I'm told, you've since been heard to mutter

Lee

(the bright blue blueprints shoved impatiently aside):

"God knows I tried,

warned him not to fly too near the sun;

but when all is done, boys will be boys,

and mine defied me. Why such a fuss?

He lived. He died. No need to sigh so

over my Absalom, my Icarus.

The ways of father and son were ever thus."

Touring in Greece

After our backpacking adventures in Crete, Joy went north to climb other mountains in Greece including Mount Parnassus, the home of the Greek gods. I headed to Patras. As it was the girls' Easter vacation, Herb drove our daughters Lisa and Hillary across the boot of Italy from Naples to Brindisi. At Brindisi they boarded the ferry to Patras where I was waiting to meet them.

The three of us spent several wonderful days in Athens exploring the Acropolis, the Parthenon, the Erechtheum, and visiting the major museums. By sheer luck we happened upon the best tour any of us has ever experienced: the Viking Tour of Greece and the Peloponnese.

Alas, Viking Tours is no more, but in 1969 Viking had the same bus, the same bus driver, and the same tour guide for the whole two-week trip. I wish I could remember the tour guide's name, as she was knowledgeable about everything: Greek

231

mythology, Greek cuisine, local flora and fauna, political history.

Perhaps the most wonderful thing about Viking Tours was its versatility. When our bus arrived at a destination, we would be given a list of places to stay, from five-star hotels to hostels for little or no cost. Another list would suggest places to find food, from elegant hotel restaurants to little hole-in-the-wall grocery shops. Thus, one could choose to travel first class or go on-the-cheap. We were of the latter variety, so we stayed in hostels. I had brought with me several metal containers and a 220-volt immersion heater, so I could make tea or soup and boil eggs. In fact, I often fed not only the three of us economically but also two young college girls who were traveling on an even smaller budget than ours.

And what wonders we visited! Early on we went to Delphi, considered by the ancients to be the *omphalos*, or navel of the world. Here was the sanctuary of Apollo as well as the seat of the Oracle of Delphi. Delphi's hillside amphitheater overlooked groves and groves of olive trees in the valley below; it could seat five thousand people.

Soon we crossed the narrow isthmus canal that bisects mainland Greece from the Peloponnese peninsula at Korinth. (Think of Paul's letters to the Corinthians.)

Next to Mycenae, Agamemnon's citadel, where we walked through the famous lion gate and saw where Homer's Argives buried their royalty with their weapons and treasure within the walls.

At Olympia we marveled at ancient olive trees and took a lap – jogging, not racing – around the oval where the original Olympic Games were held beginning in the eighth century BC. (We did not run naked as the ancient Greeks did.)

We visited the ancient fortified port city of Nafplio, thence south to Sparta before heading back to Athens.

It was such a wonderful trip that ten years later Lisa and her then boyfriend did the same Viking Tour!

Lee

Still later (almost thirty years later) in 1997 – after twelve of us had toured sacred places in Egypt and Israel – I attempted to recreate that Viking Tour with my brother Bill, who had never been to Greece. Ours was good, but not as good as Viking's.

Afterward I would write "Journey's End" for my brother.

Journey's End
(for Bill)

We sit on ancient fluted stones at Sounion Head,
And wait for sunset.
Broken columns, like the bones of fallen Titans,
Shelter small wildflowers from the wind.

The temple's standing columns soar
In stark silhouette.
Their lengthening shadows ripple over us
In waves of light and dark,
Ebbing to Poseidon's sea.

Lee

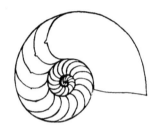

Let It Snow

Lee

Our First Ski Trip

It wasn't exactly a disaster, but it could have been. Our family of four, Lisa, Hillary, Herb and I, were living on Long Island with Herb's parents while Herb was getting some training with Sperry prior to his coming assignment to the Naval Shipyard in Bremerton, Washington. When he learned that the Sperry Ski Club had planned a ski week-end in Killington, Vermont, Herb signed the two of us up.

For one thing, we didn't have the proper clothing. I was wearing long underwear and all sorts of sweaters under a heavy Navy Pea Coat and could hardly move. (Picture a bundled-up Peanuts character.) Herb and I were both wearing baggy wool pants instead of form-fitting Lycra.

After getting outfitted in rental boots, skis and poles, we didn't have sense enough to begin with lessons. Instead, Sperry acquaintances (I won't call them friends) escorted us via chairlift to the top of an intermediate run, wished us luck, and whooshed

Lee

off down the slope. Neither Herb nor I knew how to snowplow; probably we were not even familiar with the term as applied to skiing. Somehow or other we made it down the mountain without serious injury but not without a considerable adrenaline surge. I don't remember much else about that week-end; probably we just hung out in the lodge and drank hot chocolate.

Herb realized I was intrigued, so later he treated me to a ski week in Killington in April. Because it was late in the season and the weather was unseasonably warm, the snow was soft and melting and left puddles in one's *sitzmarks*. It didn't feel *that* soft after a number of falls as the bruises on my hips would attest. But this trip came with lessons!

Ski Lessons at Snoqualmie

While we lived in Washington State, we took advantage of ski lessons with Kitsap Community College. Well, the females did: Barbara Rasmussen and her two daughters, me and my two daughters. Our husbands were both working crazy hours at the Bremerton Naval Shipyard.

Barbara and I enrolled our four pre-teen girls in a beginning class with Chuck Maiden, the portly Dean of the college. She and I signed up for an intermediate course taught by Dave Sicks, a much more elegant skier.

Graduation time came, and Barbara and I were on hand to watch our kids demonstrate their downhill stuff. What we saw had us laughing so hard we were in tears. Those four young girls skied down the hill like four smaller versions of Chuck Maiden. The style became known as the Maidenform.

Expert skier Sandy Newman offered Barbara and me free mid-week ski lessons in exchange for her lift ticket and transportation. That was a no-brainer, as Sandy was one of the most elegant skiers ever. She had qualified for her instructor's ticket when she was eight months pregnant.

At some point Sandy suggested some of us form a women's cross-country team for the 1968 Winter Olympics in Grenoble, France. At that time the United States did not have such a team. We would have had no hope of making a showing, but the experience would have been memorable. It was a pipe dream, and anyway, I had moved to Italy before such a dream could have come true.

Barb and I did go mid-week skiing with Sandy many Wednesdays. She would give us a lesson on particular skills before skiing off to do her own thing. Barb and I were becoming better skiers and gaining confidence. Then one day Sandy took us to the top of what was for us a formidable hill and assured us, "You can do it." We stood transfixed at the top of that hill for a long time, and the longer we postponed our descent the more challenging it looked.

A word about equipment. Although we would later acquire more modern boots and skis of our own, in 1965 we were still renting lace-up boots – which were rarely comfortable – and rental skis with release bindings designed to fail in case of a hard fall.

Hesitation over, Barbara announced, "I'm going!" And off she went, schussing straight down the hill, momentum carrying her clear across the wide plowed slope and into the unplowed, heavier snow where she came to a sudden stop with a full face plant.

I followed soon after, somehow managed to a stop before the heavy stuff and called out,

"Barb, are you okay?"

There was a muffled affirmative.

"Did you come out of your bindings?"

"No. But I came out of my boots."

Sure enough, there she was in her heavy wool socks, boots still securely attached to the skis.

Ski Patrol

During our five years in Italy, NATO/ NAVSUPPACT sponsored many week-end trips to ski in the Abruzzi mountains.

Eventually, the regulars decided we needed our own English-speaking Ski Patrol at Roccaraso. The Italian Alpini ski troops who served our relatively small resort were fabulous skiers and willing ski-patrolmen, but sometimes communications between English and Italian were difficult.

So Eli Iverson, the Norwegian Recreational Director arranged for the US Army Ski Patrol in Garmisch-Partenkirchen to come down from Germany to train us.

Roccaraso didn't have any really long runs, but there were some challenging ones, and those guys loved our good snow. For some strange reason, despite being further south, we had good snow longer than they did in Bavaria's Alps.

After our training, Hillary, at 15, qualified as a Junior Ski Patrol, and I managed to pass the senior test, earning an honest-to-goodness National Ski Patrol badge. My number was 007!

It Happened in St. Moritz

While living in Italy, we were fortunate to travel with NATO/NAVSUPPACT to many of the wonderful ski resorts in Europe. On this occasion, my daughter Lisa and Terry, a young Navy friend, were skiing buddies. They rode a lift to a high terminus and skied the long way down – only to find themselves not only not in St. Moritz, not even in Switzerland! They were probably in Italy.

Terry nearly panicked. "We don't even have our passports!" he moaned. (Passports were always left with the hotel staff.) My then fourteen-year-old daughter told him not to worry, they would simply find a train station and take a train back to St. Moritz.

She began asking strangers, "Where is the train station?" No one seemed to understand her English. Next she tried her school-girl French, "Ou est la gare." No recognition. She tried one of the few phrases she knew in German. "Wo ist der Bahnhof?"

Shrugs. As a last resort she ventured the Italian she was just beginning to learn: "Dove la stazione?"

"Ah!" Understanding at last, a flow of rapid Italian accompanied by lots of gesticulating. (Italians can't talk if their hands are full.) So armed with hand directions and a few numbers, she and Terry managed to find the train station and had no trouble crossing the international border on their way back to St. Moritz.

If there's a moral, it is this: all routes will eventually converge at a summit, but, of the numerous options for going down, choose carefully how you descend.

In Which I Lose My Front Teeth

During our five years in Italy (1967–1972), we spent winter week-ends skiing in the Abruzzi. After the first season Ellie Iverson, the Norwegian Recreation Director for NATO-NAVSUPPACT, asked me if I would like to teach intermediate ski classes. I would! And did. Being an instructor paid for my trips as well as those of my daughters. The tours included bus transportation, accommodations and gourmet meals at the resort Hotel Paradiso, and lift tickets. What a bonanza!

I never became an expert downhill skier, but I was competent enough to teach at the beginning or intermediate level. Among my pupils were high school kids, many enlisted men, an Admiral, an Air Force general, and two Navy doctors.

In addition to the week-end trips, NATO sponsored week-long trips to other ski resorts in Italy, Switzerland, and Germany. I was among those who got to ski in Courmayer, Cortina D'Ampezzo, Val Gardena, Sestrierre, Kitzbuhel, and St. Moritz.

In 1971 our group enjoyed a second trip to Sestrierre. On the very last day Ellie invited me to go with the better skiers to ski a black diamond run, the most challenging. By then I was confident enough to know I *could* handle it; still, I declined. I decided instead to enjoy my last few runs on a moderate, familiar slope rather than have my heart in my mouth on a really difficult course. (It always happens on the last run, right?)

So I was gliding along at a pretty fast clip, enjoying the sunny day and the kinesthetic pleasure of the skiing, when I realized I was about to overtake Matt, a young Navy medic, whom I knew to be a beginning skier. Passing him on the left or right at speed might well have spooked him, so I angled off into the deep, unplowed snow.

I have total amnesia of what followed in the next few minutes. When I regained consciousness, I was lying on my back in the snow, the young medic by my side. I don't know how he realized I had

Lee

fallen. At that point I was feeling almost no pain, but I realized my chin and mouth were bleeding. So when Matt suggested I lie back and raise my feet (to prevent shock), I said I preferred to sit up. I didn't want to choke on the blood or risk aspirating it. He thoughtfully removed his jacket and put it around me, then made his back a backrest for me until the Italian Ski Patrol arrived with the toboggan.

The two doctor friends on the tour met me at the Ski Patrol Hut and assured me I had not gone into shock. The people at the Patrol Hut referred me to the local dispensary. There they took one look at me and sent me immediately by ambulance to the hospital in Bolzano. Ellie went with me, and, because I had heard horror stories about Italian hospitals, I urged Ellie to make sure they were using sterile water and instruments. They were.

Luck was with me. Although it was a Sunday afternoon, the doctor on duty happened to be a plastic surgeon resident who did a remarkable job of restoring my chin.

I stayed in the Bolzano hospital for six days I think. The Air Force General had offered to send his plane for me. Instead, the Navy generously assigned Matt, the medic, to stay with me in Bolzano and accompany me home to Naples via a commercial flight.

There followed numerous trips to the dentist at the Naval Hospital, but eventually I had to face the fact that my front teeth couldn't be saved.

Even though Herb and I were civilians, the Navy provided me with such superior partials that they have lasted the better part of forty-five years. Thank you, US Navy!

Work and Play with Louise

In 1991, Hillary and Gray bought a property near Lambertville, New Jersey. The Lockatong place had two huge fields, a pond, a hen house, some woods, a nearly-new six-stall barn, and a not-so-new house. Hillary was teaching Equitation at Centenary College, so often there were horses in the fields or barn.

I was living alone in Maryland at the time, so when they invited me to live with them, I was pleased. I would be with family, and the rent I had been paying for my apartment in Cockeysville would be put to much better use helping with their mortgage.

Remember the saga of the five Washington Crossing roommates? Maybe I didn't tell you. The remarkable thing is that all five women delivered boy babies within a twelve-month period! (A ready-made basketball team.)

Well, that hadn't happened yet, but Louise was one of those roommates. Louise, or Weez, is a beautiful, warm, wonderful woman with an Alpha drive. It was Weez who chaired the New Hope Pennsylvania Winter Festival, who started the New Hope Nordics Ski Club, who organized the Lambertville Rowing Club. When she went into business by opening a Cross-Country Ski shop in Lambertville, she asked me to work for her.

In exchange for clerking, I got free cross-country skiing lessons as well as discounts on equipment and ski togs. Eventually I helped Weez run week-end ski trips to Vermont where she and husband Larry had a home at Mountaintop.

Several ski friends and I eventually took the week-end Amateur Ski Instructors Association course every other year. The ASIA ticket would qualify us to teach Girl Scouts, church groups or such for free.

The Nordics also sponsored cross-country ski tours: to Lake Placid, Craftsbury, Lapland Lake and other New England destinations. Once we went to

Lee

Quebec and stayed in the historic Chateau Frontenac.

My last downhill ski trip – a second one to Aspen – had been in 1976. It was wonderful to be outdoors again on snow. And what superb exercise!

Spring Skiing at Lapland Lake

An unusually warm winter:

The trails among the evergreens

Still had good snow,

But on the open, sunlit runs,

We had to skirt bare patches –

Rock outcrops and last year's grass –

Or take off skis and walk.

A line of ice melt

Ringed the edges of the lake.

Back in the lodge for lunch,

We watched our ski clothes steam

And drip,

And savored soup,

As a hundred ladybugs were busy

Hatching in the window.

Lee

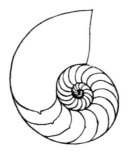

The Big Apple

Lee

New York, New York

During our five years in Italy, Herb worked as a civilian engineer with the US Navy Sixth Fleet, headquartered in Naples. I read a lot and skied a lot but worked very little. Occasionally I would substitute teach at Forest Sherman High School in whatever subject was needed: art, music, English. I did teach skiing for four of those five years, but that was in exchange for free ski trips: resort hotels, gourmet meals, lift tickets, and transportation. Not for pay.

Before we left Italy in 1972, Herb made it clear that, once we were back in the Big PX, he expected me to get a job. Again the quandary: what *could* I do? No way was I going back to teaching English with its ninety-hour work weeks!

When we returned to the States, Herb, Hillary, and I first lived in a roomy apartment in Oceanside, New York. Lisa was in school in Boston. After Hillary bailed to live with family friends in Decatur, Georgia, to finish high school there, Herb moved himself and me (and all our belongings!) in with his parents in Baldwin. And I began taking the Long Island Rail Road into Manhattan looking for work.

Herb resigned from engineering once again and went off to Charleston, South Carolina, where he felt he could write without distractions.

Meanwhile, I had actually landed a job as file clerk/legal librarian for Lauterstein and Lauterstein, a small (just three lawyers) but prestigious law firm with an impressive address: 1 Rockefeller Plaza! Since Lauterstein and Lauterstein were counsel to the Metropolitan Opera as well as its director, one of my claims to fame is that I was a witness to Sir Rudolf Bing's will. Perks included occasional tickets to the opera when one of the partners wasn't going.

Robert Lehman was another famous Lauterstein and Lauterstein client. Lehman had offered to leave his spectacular art collection to the Metropolitan Museum of Art – on condition the Met would build a special wing for it. The Met complied, and in 1975 The Robert Lehman Wing became the first addition to the Museum since it was built. And I got to attend the Grand Opening.

When I realized Herb wasn't writing or telephoning, it felt awkward to continue living with his parents – although they would have been happy to have me stay. So I rented a room and bath with kitchen privileges in a brownstone uptown near the Museum of Natural History. I wasn't making much money, but I was fulfilling a girlhood fantasy – living in New York City. There are so many extraordinary things one can do for free in the Big Apple. I loved it.

Living in the sometimes infamous City, I was determined not to live in fear. I would often go to the theater, a concert, or a movie in the evening after work, returning to 78th Street by subway late at night. Apparently appearing alert, observant, and self-confident paid off as I never ran into a problem. (Except for the time someone boarding the subway behind me clipped my heel, and my shoe fell under the train, leaving me to hobble home like *Diddle Diddle Dumpling, My Son John*.)

Lee

In June of 1963 Herb and I divorced – his idea, not mine. We remarried two months later. Ours was one of those "can't live with, can't live without" relationships. This period seemed another separation. Then Herb invited me to visit him in Charleston (a) to appreciate that city's charm and (b) to perhaps put an end to our present estrangement. *Non sequitur*: we even went clamming, a first for me.

After Herb returned to Baldwin, *magnum opus* still unwritten, he continued the courtship, coming into Manhattan, taking me out to lunch or dinner, seeking reconciliation.

I might have remained resistant had Herb not dangled before me a lure he reckoned I would find irresistible. (Made me an offer I couldn't refuse?) He was right. His new engineering assignment was to Iran, with The Imperial Iranian Air Force under the Shah. Yes!

July Fourth, 1976

Last night's Sierra Vista fireworks – viewed from the parking lot at Fry's grocery – were fun, but nothing can compare with the best Fourth of July ever.

1976 was the year of the Bicentennial. Herb and Hillary were staying with Herb's parents on Long Island. I was living uptown in Manhattan, Lisa downtown in the Village. We all convened in Baldwin on the evening of July third.

Early on the morning of the Fourth we drove the Beltway along the southern shore of Long Island, under the Verrazano Bridge into Brooklyn to Manhattan. Our land route paralleled the progress of the "tall ships" as they arrived and sailed under the Verrazano Bridge, into New York Harbor and up the Hudson River.

Participants in the 1976 Parade of Ships:

Amerigo Vespucci (Italy)   *Christian Radich* (Norway)
Barba Negra (Norway)   *Danmark* (Denmark)

Lee

Dar Pomorza (Poland)	*Mircea* (Romania)
Eagle (USA)	*Nippon Maru* (Japan)
Esmeralda (Chile)	*Regina Maris* (USA)
Gloria (Colombia)	*Sagres* (Portugal)
Gorch Fock (Germany)	*Sebbe Als* (Denmark)
Juan Sebastián de Elcano (Spain)	*T/S Te Vega* (Panama)
	Peyk (Turkey)
Kruzenshtern (Soviet Union)	*Roseway* (USA)
Libertad (Argentina)	*Transition* (USA)

"Tall ships" are the three-masted sailing ships which most of the world's navies employ as training vessels for young seamen. To celebrate our Bicentennial at least twenty of them, representing fourteen different countries, sailed into New York.

Herb found a parking space near where I was living – a difficult matter any time – a remarkable feat on this holiday! From there we walked crosstown to the park on Riverside Drive, with a ringside seat for the Parade. We watched President Ford sail by on the *Eagle* and receive salutes from all the other ships.

We had fortified ourselves with New York bagels, loaded with cream cheese, lox, and Bermuda onion slices, and which we enjoyed while watching the spectacle. And the spectacle was spectacular.

That evening the four of us rode the over-crowded subway (standing room only) south to Battery Park to watch the fireworks. It was like a Chinese New Year on steroids. Was there ever in history such a glorious display?

Lee

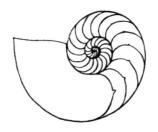

Persia

Lee

Yogurt

In 1978, when Herb accepted a civilian engineering assignment with the Imperial Iranian Air Force, we fully expected a house. What we got was one room in a BOQ. One room with two *single* beds, no closet, and a Turkish toilet (a hole in the floor). On one bed we stashed our skis, SCUBA gear, mountain-climbing equipment, our portable kitchen and traveling library, plus our summer and winter clothing. Herb and I slept spoon-fashion in the other single bed.

Life became more reasonable once we were allotted a second room and could prepare our own food. On one of our forays to Tehran – fourteen hours by Land Rover – we acquired a small refrigerator which helped immensely.

The village of Abdanan (not Abadan), was about half a mile away from the base. It had not changed much from its days as a goat-hair tent settlement whose residents traded by muleback over the border with Iraq. Often the only available food in the village was dessicated potatoes, cabbage, or green beans which had been trucked in over hot dusty roads. On one occasion we did manage to purchase a scrawny chicken, once the villager understood our repeated Farsi "Morgh. Morgh." Now and then there was lamb or goat meat at the base commissary, but it was good only for stew. No such thing as a lamb chop.

Whenever we ate at the Officers' Mess, I would inevitably end up with Turkish tummy. Well, no surprise. There was little or no sanitation and no screens, so flies were rampant; and the cooks were uneducated draftees with little notion of cleanliness.

One *could* get yogurt in the village. It was sold across a wooden counter in a three-sided hut with a dirt floor. Somehow the yogurt man knew about dispensing it in pristine plastic bags. How did the yogurt get from the vat into the bags? By the shop-owner scooping his cup wrist-deep into the vat. (Sometimes it's best to suspend one's belief in the germ theory.)

Doubtless that yogurt was made from goat's milk and cooked over a goat-dung fire, but after a while it tasted ever so much better than the pasteurized product we occasionally got in Tehran. I'm convinced that delicious goat-milk yogurt helped keep me healthy those two years.

Lee

A Letter from Abdanan

Two days ago, between the radar site and base,
A ghastly sight: our mountain road
All red with blood.
Alive
With writhing bodies.
No, not the grisly carnage of a traffic accident.
Not in this isolated spot – fourteen hours
By Land Rover from Tehran. Rather, nomads
Slaughtering some seventeen or twenty sheep
Or goats – to be consumed, we assumed,
By guests at rustic wedding feast:
Conspicuous consumption Kurdish style.

Then yesterday the vultures.
A dozen perhaps.
We saw no tearing, rending, flailing,
No frenzied gorging on the waste.
They perched, remote and regal,
On rocks to wait our passing.
Robed in gray. Awesome, clean, and

Strangely beautiful.
Huge birds! Half the size of us!
Stately giants beside our ravens,
The omnipresent poor who daily caw our sky.
These were creatures of legend,
Improbable as Rocs or Phoenixes.

Today, bleached bones, sweet-smelling air,
A scene again serene.
The somber visitors had done their work and gone,
Trailing only Khayyam echoes,
"Ah, whence, and whither flown again, who knows!"

Wherever vultures go, we here and now invoke
A blessing on these creatures,
A blessing on all scavengers.
Inshallah! Mashallah!
God willing. God be praised.

Almost Arrested by SAVAK

In 1978, Herb and I were living in Abdanan, Iran, in Bachelor Officer's Quarters, on a remote Imperial Iranian Air Force Base. An Air Force Base without so much as a runway – only a heliport – but one with a BIG radar for spying over the Iraqi border. We were fourteen hours from Tehran by Land Rover over a mountain pass and a dirt road, six hours from the nearest telephone – which might or might not work – and where our mail took weeks if it came or went at all.

By the time of this incident we had acquired a second room in the BOQ, one for sleeping and gear, the other for cooking and entertaining. Our guests were the two English-speaking Pakistani doctors or, now and then, a few of the young Irani officers who had trained in Texas and were eager to practice their English. (They were always interrogated after visiting us.)

Herb had to do all the maintenance on our big, green, ancient Land Rover. He needed some parts, so we drove to Dezful, the nearest town that might have auto parts.

I soon became bored with car talk in two languages, so told Herb I'd be taking some pictures in town. I took a wonderful photo of a row of intestinal bladders for carrying liquids that looked ever so like a row of nursing piglets – however unlikely piglets in a Moslem country.

Before long I became aware that I had attracted the attention of two well-dressed young men. Well, what was one to expect? A Western woman in a Moslem country without an escort and not wearing a chador? I knew not to make eye contact and went on looking for subjects for my camera. I spotted a really interesting-looking, wrinkled but bright-eyed elderly woman.

Aware that many easterners do not want their image "stolen," I very carefully pointed to the camera, then to her with a question on my face. She understood immediately and seemed delighted at the idea. In her long black chador she smiled for me and the camera, then called over an elder male for me to take his picture, too.

By then the two young men were getting uncomfortably close, so I headed back to the automotive shop and Herb. They followed. I saw the automotive clerk turn pale when the three of us entered the shop. The young men began asking Herb and me for our papers. Not rudely, but insistently. Fortunately, our passports and Visas were in order. Even more fortunately, we both had official military identification by virtue of Herb's contract with the Imperial Iranian Air Force. Eventually, via a mixture of Farsi (of Persian) and English, we gathered that they thought I was ridiculing the oldsters – and, by extension, making fun of their relatively backward country.

Nothing could have been further from the truth. But how could I explain that I had been charmed by the elderly lady, thrilled to encounter someone so utterly different from me.

It seems our papers satisfied the two young men – obviously representatives of SAVAK, the secret police, comparable to the KGB. And we did not get arrested.

Only on the way back to the base in Abdanan did we realize what a close call that may have been. SAVAK would not have needed a reason to detain us. We could have just "disappeared." And, given our isolation, it might have been months before we were missed – missed seriously enough to begin an investigation.

Lee

Fishing and Tea in Iran

Our daughters, Lisa and Hillary, came to visit Herb and me in Iran in 1978. As Herb and I were living in two small rooms in a BOQ at a remote Imperial Iranian Air Force Base (with a heliport but no runway), I can't remember where they slept. It's possible one of the Pakistani doctors moved in with the other and offered his room to the girls.

Anyway, Dr. Younas (Jonah) and Dr. Baktawar proposed a fishing excursion as a treat during the girls' visit. They hired a four-wheeled vehicle, and the six of us took off through rough, barren country which seemed to lack any semblance of a road or track. They must have known where we were going as, eventually, we arrived at a good-sized river, and the Pakistanis began to fish.

Their system of fishing consisted of throwing exploding sticks of dynamite into the river. Naturally, they got their catch but at the cost of hundreds of other dead fishes and river life. It was hard for the females to hide their dismay.

The day was beastly hot, probably well over a hundred degrees Fahrenheit, with no shade in sight; so the girls and I shed the slacks and long-sleeved shirts we had been wearing over our swimsuits and began floating down the river, still wearing our hats and sunglasses.

In some way, mysterious to us, the Pakistanis had arranged for us to have tea with a Kurdish family. Though they spoke different languages, they managed to communicate in Urdu. We sat on a gorgeous Persian rug under the shade of the black tent's overhang, where the patriarch served us dark sweet tea. We took turns drinking from their one china cup. Maybe just one cup but this was a very wealthy group; one had only to note the number of their sheep and goats.

The Kurdish womenfolk were not to be seen (and our daughters probably didn't count), but when Dr. Younas asked our host if his family felt honored to have an American couple visit, the old man was clearly taken aback.

I was wearing a hat, a shirt, and long pants, and he hadn't realized I was a woman!

Well, of course the women had been listening, and, overcome with curiosity, began peeking through the tent opening. Then a huge woman I assumed to be the matriarch actually made an entrance wearing a floor-length dress of dark, green plush and sporting a gold incisor. Her horny, calloused feet were testimony to the many miles she walks barefoot each year in the tribe's migrations. This formidable woman clasped me in her strong arms and said what must have been the Kurdish equivalent of *Mashallah!* (God bless!) To say it was a magical moment is a vast understatement.

Sightseeing in Iran

In 1979 when Herb's tour with the Iranian Air Force was over, we wanted to see some of Persia's historic places before leaving the country.

On a miserably hot day we stopped at an archaeological site and museum in ancient Susa, now Shush, where we were the only visitors. The guy in the parking lot, hoping for a big tip for guarding our car, handed me a piece of what we both thought was bone. It turned out to be part of a small archaic horse with a saddle, probably dating from BCE. A similar, more complete one resides in the National Archaeological Museum in Tehran.

When we left Abdanan, we were aware that there had been riots in Tabriz but had no inkling it was the beginning of the revolution.

Our timing was propitious. Herb and I departed Iran without incident. Later that year a number of friends and colleagues had to leave the country with just an overnight bag, having to

Lee

abandon Persian rugs, automobiles, and family photographs.

Our tour included the Tomb of Cyrus the Great and the ancient capital of Persepolis. In 1971 Persepolis celebrated the 2,500th anniversary of the founding of the Persian Empire. Those visits inspired the two poems that follow.

Panoply

All around Persepolis
The stocky soldiers march:
Mede and Persian, Persian Mede,
They line each wall and arch.

Solemn, in costumed majesty,
Each decked out like a chief,
They guard the courtyards, climb the stairs,
In rigid bas-relief.

There, still hold fast the forms of duty.
Rank and file advance
In frozen rhythm, profile stance,
Without one backward glance.

Lee

Mede and Persian, Persian Mede,
Brother follows brother
So uniformly well turned out
One looks just like another.

They seem at first identical,
Stamped from a common mold,
But graved above each soldier's head
His private number's told.

As if he might have mentioned, "Wife,
Tomorrow with the sun,
Look for me on the eastern gate,
Position two-six-one."

All around Persepolis,
In company or lone,
Loyal Medes and Persians march
Stolidly in stone.

Pasagardae

Morning on the Morghab Plain,
We make a pilgrimage.

Here Cyrus was victorious
(Before there was a Periclean Greece or Golden Age),
Here built his capital,
And here began to fuse a Persian Empire
That would range from Egypt to the Indus.
And here his tomb.
Great Cyrus rests not here.
His bones were scattered long before
That upstart Alexander came to pay him homage,
Came, and knelt, and wept.

Lee

A spare serenity pervades this place.
The plinth is monumental, grand –
So steep we climb on hands and knees –
The lintel low.
(One makes, perforce, obeisance to the king.)
Inside,
Only emptiness,
Cold stones worn smooth,
A hollow hush.
Still, in that stillness
Small hairs rise to attention,
Ears seem to hear eroded graven words,
A silence shouting down the centuries:

"I AM KURUSH, THE KING, THE ACHAEMENIAN...."

(The shahinshah, the king of kings.)

"Nothing beside remains."

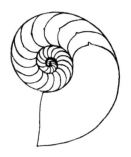

South America

Lee

On My Own

One of the most satisfying trips was my 1979 journey through South America. It was particularly satisfying, because I accomplished that trip totally on my own – no tour group, no traveling companion, no reservations – just a tentative itinerary. And, fortunately, no problems – other than a bit of altitude sickness at 16,000 feet on the train to Huancayo in Peru.

It came about like this: when Herb got his assignment to work with the Argentinian Air Force in Buenos Aires, they wanted him there "yesterday." Westinghouse would pay for my airfare, but I declined to accompany him. "No. No. No," said I. "I want to *see* something on the way."

It turned out my ticket allowed me multiple stops between Baltimore and Buenos Aires – as long as I didn't backtrack. It took me a month or more to reach Buenos Aires; on the way I visited four countries: Colombia, Bolivia, Ecuador, and Peru.

Lee

After Herb completed his tour in Argentina, he and I visited friends in Chile which made it six South American countries for me. Actually eight if you count the short stops we made in Paraguay and Brazil on our trip to Iguazu Falls.

Trains, planes, cars, buses, and boats were all involved.

My favorite South American destination has to be Machu Picchu in Peru, a site I would revisit twice. I'm proud to say I climbed Big Brother, the higher peak there.

Machu Picchu is one of those magical places on the planet, an energy vortex such as the ones at Easter Island in the Pacific, Ayers Rock in Australia, Lhasa in Tibet, Avebury in England - a site similar to but older than Stonehenge. Arizona has one, in Sedona.

South American Superlatives

*The gold exhibit and ancient coin collection
in* Bogota *have no rivals.*

In Ecuador, *it's fun to stand with one foot
in each hemisphere.*

When you fly into La Paz,
*you land in "Peace" –
and at the highest airport on the planet.*

On Lake Titicaca
*you can walk on water. (Sorta.)
If your boat lets you off
onto a living, floating island
(a sort of Sargasso Sea),
where they make reed boats,
you'll dip and bob with every step.*

Lee

The train from Lima *to* Huancayo *crosses the Andes.*
A pass at sixteen thousand feet
makes it the highest railroad in the world.
You can find a wonderful, warm, wool poncho
at Huancayo's marvelous Indian market.

The Foz do Iguazu
(which border Argentina, Paraguay, and Brazil)
Put Victoria and Niagara to shame.
One can see full-circle rainbows there.

Argentina's Rio Gallegos *has forty foot tides,*
tides that can leave large boats alist.

After you watch glaciers calving in Los Glaciares,
continue south across the Strait of Magellan
into Tierra del Fuego.
There, on the Beagle Canal, you'll find Ushuaia,
the continent's southernmost city.

In Chile, visit Valparaiso, *and experience Paradise.*

The Nazca Lines

Inscribed on the desert in Peru,
and almost inaccessible,
Are curious designs: a candelabrum, spider,
Monkey, hummingbird, a condor flying –
All drawn with delightful rendering of form,
Economy of line.
The monkey's tail winds in a spiral,
Coiled like a spring, a seashell, or a maze.

Some straight lines line up with the sun at solstice
But of such length, on such a scale,
The mind can scarcely comprehend:
The space embraced within the monkey's arms
May measure forty meters.

The scope and range of other figures there
Combine to form a complex so complex
A ground observer,
Standing in the pupil of the condor's eye,
Or poised upon his primary tip

Lee

(In line to be struck by hummingbird bill),
Would not perceive the pattern.
No, only from the air.

Who etched the desert there?
Who solved that intricate geometry and supervised
Inscribing it in stone?
And why? Are these figures
Runways for the chariots of the gods?
Signposts for some fellow stellar travelers?
Whimsically decorated irrigation ditches?
An astronomical calendar in litho?
A prehistoric fable, petrified?

Are we expected to believe
that pre-Colombian Indians
Who never learned to write,
Who never managed to invent the wheel,
Conceived such plans
And gouged the Nazca Lines
for watchers in the sky?

Inca Walls

In Cuzco, in Hostal Loreto,
while adjusting to the altitude,
you may sleep in a room with an Inca wall –
even rest your hand against it.

Some stones at Sacsahuaman
(they withstand earthquakes)
weigh as much as three hundred tons,
yet their puzzle pieces fit so perfectly –
without benefit of mortar –
a playing card won't slip between.

At Machu Picchu,
on the now unjungled terraces
Hiram Bingham happened on a century ago,
I lean against an Inca wall.
A bright bromeliad leans out.

Lee

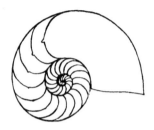

Argentina

Lee

Quinta "El Conejito"

When Herb and I arrived in Argentina in 1979, the country was in turmoil. President Juan Peron had died in 1974. (His beloved wife Eva Peron "Evita" had died in 1952.) Peron was succeeded by his second wife, Isabel, affectionately called "Isabelita."

Isabel soon lost favor and power, and in 1976 a right-wing *coup d'etat* overthrew her. A military junta was installed to replace her, and dissent was silenced.

Inflation was rampant. (The Inflation Rate in Argentina averaged 202.25 percent from 1944 until 2016. It reached an all time high of 20,262.80 percent in March of 1990.) Banks were failing.

Worse, people began "disappearing." The military was kidnapping, torturing and/or killing anyone suspected of being less than loyal to the regime.

Lee

Matters were difficult for Argentinians. Not so much for us. Herb was a civilian working for the Argentinian Air Force whose personnel appreciated him. I took Spanish lessons, read all the Faulkner available in the American library, and adopted a cat. I called her "Carboncita" as she was rescued from the coal merchants who would have killed her.

We lived in Moreno, a suburb of Buenos Aires, in a rented *quinta,* called El Conejito or "Little Rabbit". The definition of *quinta* as a country estate or villa is misleading. Ours was a very simple, unheated, one-bedroom house. As in Italy, we had to rely on Alladin (kerosene) heaters to manage in winter.

There was another building on the property – whose name I forget – dominated by a gigantic fireplace for roasting meat or *asado*. Steaks were very big in Argentina. Herb once roasted a whole suckling pig there. The building had tables and chairs enough to entertain twenty or more people.

Reflections

While living in Argentina, I wrote about the cat and the seasons. And I composed a villanelle for Las Locas de Mayo, the Crazy Women of the Plaza de Mayo, who bravely challenged the junta. Between 1977 and 1983 they demonstrated in public places in ever-growing numbers to protest the missing, demanding to know what happened to their husbands, brothers, or sons.

Lee

Look What Followed Me Home
(in the trunk of the car)

Sweetheart, look at this kitten I brought home to eat.
She was frightened and hungry,
left to die in the street.
> *Well, I'll cook it, but, really,*
> *there won't be much meat.*

I'll just give her some milk.
See how sweetly she begs?
> *Yes. For liver and beefsteak,*
> *for fish and fresh eggs.*
> *And later she'll claw up the furniture legs.*

Curled up by the fire. Just what could be neater?
> *Now she's finished with feeding,*
> *she's hogging the heater.*
> *No wonder she's sleepy;*
> *she laps cream by the liter.*

She's so grateful and loving. What a leonine purr!

Always nuzzling and rubbing.

Only grooming her fur.

And wait till she yowls nights.

*Then **I'll** play the cur.*

Inside or outside, cats never leave messes.

They carefully cover up whatever passes.

(And afterwards, carefully, they lick their asses.)

Her fur is so soft, and it's groomed to a sheen.

She's so cute when she washes. Cats really are clean.

You're forgetting my work clothes

were once her latrine.

Entertaining?

She'll perform with a prune pit for hours.

Next thing, you'll be saying

she has magic powers.

And just how will you feel

when she digs up your flowers?

Lee

How muscular cats are! How taut and alert!
Or else so completely relaxed they're inert.
>   *You'd forgive her for shredding*
>   *your stockings or skirt.*

Leaping six times her height!
She defies Newton's Laws!
Yet tracks safely through trinkets.
Such well-designed paws.
>   *Such cute padded sheaths,*
>   *hiding such lethal claws!*

She's as agile and lithe as the waves on the ocean.
A Markova in action. A poem in motion.
>   *And she **may** let you pet her –*
>   *if **she** takes the notion.*

Cats are as swift and as graceful as arrows.
>   *Yes, I've seen how she stealthily*
>   *lengthens and narrows,*
>   *Preparing to pounce upon unwary sparrows.*

Cats can be useful. They catch mice, you know.
 So I've been told. How they pounce, then let go.
  How they tease before killing.
  They put on quite a show.

How expressive her eyes are! She can practically talk.
And gregarious? She follows wherever I walk.
 Cats are glinty-eyed, disloyal loners who stalk!

Great authors and poets have taken their part.
Cats are models for yoga; they're models for art
She's delightful. I like her. Come on, have a heart!

 Say, I'm not Santa Claus.
 And it's not Christmas, is it?
 And no cat is my notion of something exquisite.
 Still, I guess she can stay. **But just for a visit!**

 (Carboncita, I concede you're entitled to nap,
  Since you captured the mouse
 that eluded the trap.
 But let's not let HER know
 I've allowed you my lap.)

Lee

Invierno

El vendedor de kerosene
Cuando anda va en carro;   No contesta el caballo.
Dos ruedas colorados,   E resopla humo blanco
Un caballo grande, pardo.   Y patea en la calle
                             Haciendo resonar
Desde lejos escuchamos   la calle duro (Duro como
Su ruido, su clamor.   si fuera hierro).
En voz alta llama   Como campana resuena.
"Ke-ro, Ke-ro-SE-ne!"   Yo afuera hace Frio,
Va llamando acercamo.   Sopla el viento.
                             Es invierno.
Paran ellos. con mi cubo   Aca, adentro de la casa
Voy y pido   Nos acercamoos

"Kerosene, por favor."   A la estufa,
El vendedor mi cubo llena   Gozando mucho
Entretando, hablo yo   De su calor.
a su caballo.   Gracias al vendedor.

Winter

When the kerosene man fills my pail.
makes his rounds, Meanwhile, I talk
he comes in a cart to his horse.
with two red wheels
[drawn by] one large, The horse doesn't answer,
dark horse. He puffs white smoke
and stamps [his hoof]
From far away [on] the [dirt] road,
we [can] hear his making the iron-hard road
noise and shouting. resound,
Loudly he calls, clang like a bell.
"Ke-ro, Ke-ro-SE-ne!" Already it's cold outside.
Goes on calling The wind is blowing.
coming closer. It's winter.
Here, inside the quinta
They arrive. we draw close to the
With my pail heater, enjoying the
I go [out] and ask for warmth. Thanks to
"Kerosene, please." the kerosene man.
The kerosene man

Lee

Verano

Ah!
Mira!
Que cerca
Parecen las
Estrellas esta
Noche tan hermosa!
Titilan las luciernagas.

Summer

Oh!

Look!

How close

The stars seem

This beautiful night!

Fireflies are twinkling

Lee

Villanelle Por Las Locas de Mayo

Most of us never learn to live with fear.
We stay cocooned from ills that might have been.
What terror theirs whose loved-ones disappear!

For most, the gradual decay from year
To year is worst of threats to friends or kin.
Most of us never learn to live with fear.

A bump at night may interrupt our cheer,
May prompt a moment's prickling of the skin.
What terror theirs whose loved-ones disappear!

We call such happenings tragic, think them queer,
Are glad they never happen here. But then,
Most of us never learn to live with fear.

Far kinder certain death of someone dear

Than dread unknowns,

than deathless hopes grown thin.

What terror theirs whose loved-ones disappear!

Not ours the thudding heart, the straining ear,

The sleepless eye, the breath too long held in.

Most of us never learn to live in fear.

What terror theirs whose loved-ones disappear!

(Argentina, 1980)

Lee

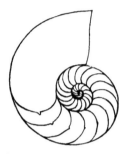

Maryland

Lee

Ah! Wilderness

For a number of years Herb and I owned a bit of wilderness. Our particular wilderness was a seven-acre ridge in a dedicated forest preserve in Patrick County, Virginia, just off the Blue Ridge Parkway. At one time the Appalachian Trail ran past it. Our ridge has since become part of Busted Rock, a luxury resort in the Blue Ridge.

We never built a cabin on the property. Our only improvements were a lean-to, a sleeping platform for out tent, and a raised fireplace. The family did enjoy camping and picnicking there.

One autumn Herb decided he and I should survey it. So we did! Afterwards Herb even made a three-dimensional topographical map of the place. (I wonder what became of that map.)

A rock, blasted in creating the Appalachian Trail, gave the area its name: "Busted Rock." A geodetic benchmark on that busted rock gave us the bearing we needed for accurate measurements.

Lee

Daughter Lisa has pointed out that my description of the project incidentally contains double portraits – of my husband and me.

Height-Finding at Busted Rock

There we are, the pair of us,
Undertaking to measure the earth –
Or a goodly parcel thereof –
Inchworms sizing it up and down,
Playing King of the Mountain, reigning
Monarchs of all we survey.

Your quick, trained eye aims slowly,
Sights precisely,
Focusing down the dark enclosure
Along a solitary ray,
And finds its fine and distant mark.
You so remark.

Meanwhile my gaze encompasses all the angles,
Ranges through the azimuths from
Brown to green to blue and back again,
And by degrees
Observes the curves of lichens on a log.

Lee

It wanders random,
Random as the trailing cedar trails.

Yours is the straight and narrow
Search for truth, through knowledge, numbers,
Notes recorded in a book.
Thus, one transient with a transit
(Have tripod; will travel)
Becomes cartographer, a charter of courses.
You plot in abstract symbols
The lay of the land.
That's your way of drawing it close,
Of holding it in your hand.

Mine is to fondle the actual dirt.
As keeper of the rod, I have time to keep in touch.
I stand patiently at my appointed place,
A friend to (akin to) the terrapin,
A watcher of warblers,
A smeller of mosses,
Now nestled in the dusty rhododendrons,

Now clinging vinelike to some sapling

Under a rain of yellow stars.

I wave my wand: Hello, World!

I wave my wand so you can find me

(Wherever it is I am).

I'm found. We mark the spot:

You in the book,

I on the ground,

Disturbing how many years of leaf-fall.

Note how

– and by what divergent paths –

We arrive at the same site. Exploring

Downhill slopes and ascending elevations,

At bottom we reach new heights,

For where the fall-lines merge,

We find fresh-welling sources

Springing forth.

Lee

Some later time,

Some other undertaking,

Some other plot of earth (or fire, or water)

Will there be a moment to recall

How we took to the October air there,

And found our spring in fall?

Private Pilots

Getting a flying license was unfinished business for Herb after a hearing loss kept him out of the Navy V-12 Flight Program his Freshman year at Duke.

So, while we lived in Italy, he took lessons through the NATO Flying Club and earned his ticket.

After one of the would-be pilots clipped a wing – driving an airplane as if it were an automobile – the Club ordered a new Cessna. Herb was one of the Club members who took the train to Germany to pick it up. And he was one of the lucky pilots who got to fly it back to Italy over the Alps at a relatively low altitude.

Later, back in the States, Herb became the owner of half an airplane. Naturally, our daughters wanted to know, "Which half? Top or bottom? Left or right? Front or back?"

While we lived in Maryland, Herb treated me to flying lessons. Joe, my instructor, was a grizzled old codger who had filled many, many flight-log books. We flew out of Fallston, Maryland in a Cessna 150. The small airport had no tower, so I didn't get much practice in radio communications; it was a see-and-be-seen operation for take-offs and landings.

I have taken many examinations in my life: I passed the Graduate Record Exam easily, aced the National Teacher Exam, even qualified for Mensa, but far and away the most difficult test for me was passing the FAA written exam. It was full of critical technical and numerical material that one had to be responsible for, and I am a word person, not a numbers person.

But pass it I did. Then began a series of solo flights both locally and to unfamiliar airports. Solo flights often necessitated communications with various towers and required changing radio frequencies. Once I had to avoid the restricted zone around Camp David. Eventually I had my flight test with an inspector in the co-pilot's seat. Mine included simulating an engine failure, locating an emergency landing area, and landing safely on it. I passed that one, too.

Once I was licensed, Herb had me do some night flights to unfamiliar airports. One day I flew to New Jersey and took daughter Hillary for a short flight. Next was a longer flight from Maryland to North Carolina where I gave my mother a view from the air of her Greensboro area. After that I never flew solo.

Instead, I became an accomplished co-pilot. Herb realized his ataxia would eventually prevent his being able to pass the physical, but he could continue to fly as long as there was a licensed pilot aboard.

I got pretty good at knowing where we were in relation to the map or by dead reckoning. I could spot the Omnidirectional Radio Beacons that would flip the compass when you flew over them, thus assuring you you were on course.

Herb and I made some wonderful flying trips together. We took in October foliage in New

Lee

England; there was a week-long trip to Florida, with stops at Lake Okeechobee and in Miami, where we visited friends and the duplexes we had built.

One of the most memorable ones I've described in "Night Flight."

Night Flight

My grandmother used to say
her grandmother used to say,
"Comparisons are odious."

At risk of disturbing either's rest
I offer this superlative:
the flight that really was the best.

It began in the afternoon when
after work, Herb wanted to do some work
on the plane.
He owned half a Cessna then.
The girls wanted to know which half,
Front? Bottom? Starboard side?
I came along with a book.

When Herb finished the job,
he stretched and said, "Look!"
So I looked,

Lee

and beheld – as if balanced on the rudder –
the red-orange Harvest moon.

Herb did a quick pre-flight;
I undid the tie-downs,
and, after run-up and control checks,
we were off!

In the air,
Herb contacted JFK Departure Control
to see if they could read our transponder transmission.
They couldn't,
so we couldn't transit the TCA.

Instead, we flew above it,
west from Long Island, avoiding Kennedy,
banked right, and followed the Hudson upstream,
flying VFR at eighty-five hundred.

It was an aviator's

– it was an I love New York'er's –

dream.

The bright moonlight shone

on the New York City we love to love:

the Statue of Liberty, the Narrows Bridge,

World Trade Towers, Chrysler Building,

Empire State, Rockefeller Center,

St. Patrick's Cathedral, Columbus Circle,

Lincoln Center (not named for Abraham),

the city laid out like a grid around

the huge dark swath of Central Park. In the Bronx,

past the graceful George Washington Bridge,

a game was in progress at Yankee Stadium.

What a night! Bright as day.

What a magic carpet ride.

I can say – with some Authority –

it took us a long time to come down to earth.

How Suzan Changed My Life

Girls in my generation didn't have the opportunity to do much in the way of sports. Oh, we had the compulsory half hour of "gym," when we had to wear those awful yellow bloomers, and in grammar school we played at basketball and baseball, neither of which I was good at. As a teen, I considered myself clumsy, a clutz prone to trip over the pattern in the rug.

My opinion was reinforced when, in my Freshman year of college, a "C" in field hockey kept me off Dean's List. Fortunately for me, Duke required only one group sport, so after field hockey I chose more individual Phys Ed courses such as modern dance and swimming. Swimming I took to. By Senior year I had earned my Red Cross Water Safety Instructor badge which in turn earned me the position of Waterfront Director at both Girl Scout and YWCA summer camps at Crabtree Creek State Park. (Alas, Crabtree Creek lost its charming name and became Umpstead State Park to honor a governor.)

Fast forward thirty years – a husband and two children later. Now I'm fifty, and I considered myself reasonably fit – until daughter Hillary, who was visiting, challenged me to run around the quarter-mile track at the high school; I was startled to find myself winded after just that fourth of a mile. So I signed up for the free group tennis classes sponsored by the Baltimore County recreation department. I never got very good at tennis, but I did enjoy it, so when one of the women in the class asked if I wanted to continue meeting and hitting some balls, I agreed enthusiastically.

One day, as we were leaving the courts, Suzan turned to me and said, "You know, I've been trying for three years to run the Lady Equitable five kilometer race, and I can't seem to get through the winter training. I think if I had a buddy, I'd be more likely to make it. Interested?"

I was emphatically *not* interested and told her so. But when I got home I thought to myself, "Gee, Pam, she's your friend. It wouldn't kill you to train with her." So I phoned Suzan and agreed to be her training partner.

That agreement was a good thing. The Lady Equitable is an early spring race, so one must train through the winter. Many a morning one of us would say, "Do we *have* to do this today?" and the other would reply "Yes, we do! We're going to *do* this thing if we have to do it on our hands and knees!" So Suzan and I jogged on – in the rain, in the sleet, in the wind, in the snow, on icy roads.

By mid-winter Suzan's sister-in-law, Cora, had also signed on. Now Suzan was ten years younger than me, and Cora was ten years younger than Suzan, so we had three different target times for when we hoped to finish.

I no longer remember what our target times were, but all three of us came in under our target times! At the finish line I was so spent, I could barely lift my arm to put it into the sleeve of the down parka husband Herb was holding for me. But oh the exhilaration! What a high!

With the Lady Equitable completed, Suzan had accomplished her goal and never ran again. But I was hooked. Eventually I completed three marathons: Maryland when I was fifty-three, New York when I was sixty, and Philadelphia when I was seventy.

Moral: You just never know what might result when you agree to help a friend.

Three Marathons

Baltimore's Maryland Marathon is called "The Mean One," because Satyr Hill, the steepest portion of the course, occurs at the eighteen-mile mark, the point where most runners hit the glycogen wall. That's when the glycogen stores in the liver and muscles are depleted resulting in energy drain and fatigue.

I hadn't exactly planned to run the Maryland Marathon; in 1983 I had been running for only a couple years. I had done a lot of 5k's, several 10k's, and two ten-mile races, so I was ready for the next challenge. The next challenge would be a half marathon or thirteen miles. To make it real, I signed up for the Maryland one, aware that it was an out-and-back course, thus easy to bail at Pierce's Plantation, the half-way point.

My longest training run had been eighteen miles, so I was confident I could do thirteen; but, after pulling an Achilles tendon, I backed way off the training.

The day of the race was beautiful, I was feeling fine, and Herb would be waiting at the halfway station. Early on I identified a runner ahead of me going about my pace, so I fell into step behind her – until we got to Satyr Hill where she left me in the dust as I opted to *walk* up Satyr Hill. The conservation of energy paid off; it wasn't long before I passed that pace-setter.

At Pierce's Plantation I waved to Herb, turned around, and ran on. When he met me at the finish, I said I wanted to stay for the results. When they were announced, I had won first place in my category: female runners over fifty! It took me six hours, 20 minutes.

Often distance runners are so sore after a race they can hardly walk afterward and must back down stairs the next day. I felt so good I ran six miles the day after the marathon. Exhilaration is a powerful stimulant.

Lee

X   X   X

Probably the most exciting marathon is New York City's. Boston may be more prestigious, but New York is the world's largest – with over 50,000 finishers. It is so large that getting to run it is by lottery or by qualifying. My showing in Maryland plus my age (I was sixty) took care of the entry. The New York Marathon runs through all five of New York City's boroughs. Runners convene at the New York Public Library (by the lions) around 3:00 in the morning whence they are bused to Staten Island. There they try to stay warm, jogging gently, stretching, or bundled up in layers inside tents.

The race begins on Staten Island in waves around 10:00, elite runners first, the rest grouped by anticipated finish time so no one gets trampled. From Staten Island the route crosses the Verrazano Narrows Bridge into Brooklyn, thence into Queens, goes across the Queensboro Bridge into Manhattan, then north to the Bronx before turning south in Manhattan, all the way to Columbus Circle, finally finishing in Central Park.

While runners are crossing the nearly two-and-a-half miles of the Verrazano Narrows Bridge (13,700 feet), fireboats on the Hudson are spouting red white and blue plumes of water. As the runners get warm, they begin shedding those extra layers they needed on Staten Island. All that clothing will be collected by the New York Road Runners and given to the homeless.

On that first Sunday in November the bridge is closed to vehicular traffic, and both the upper and lower levels are filled with those fifty thousand runners. Once on land the thousands of runners are outnumbered by the millions of spectators who line both sides of the route and cheer the runners on. The enthusiasm of the crowds gives an added boost to a runner's high.

The route goes through a number of ethnic neighborhoods, little Puerto Rico, Black Harlem, Spanish Harlem; and Hasidic Jews are out in their side curls and beaver hats. Latinos play music at the dreaded eighteen-mile mark.

Timing is done electronically; runners' chips register every five kilometers as well as at the finish, so one can know one's time down to the second. My finish time was 6:24:20. The exhilaration outweighs the exhaustion.

X   X   X

The Philadelphia Marathon is special because the route passes so many iconic landmarks of our history: Independence Hall, Betsy Ross House, the Liberty Bell, City Hall (William Penn atop). The course passes along the charming streets of Old City on Penn's Landing by the Delaware River, eventually arriving near the green and leafy pathways of the Fairmount Water Works, located on the Schuylkill River.

The race begins and terminates at the Philadelphia Museum of Art, famous for all those steps which *Rocky Balboa* raced up. No, we didn't have to negotiate the steps, but it was a great place for friends and family to sit and watch the finish.

Runners are supposed to finish the Philadelphia Marathon in under seven hours. Tara Burgy, my running buddy, and I did not.

Though the course was technically closed – and all the water stations packed up and gone – Tara and I knew the route and persevered through Manayunk dodging pedestrian and automobile traffic before turning south back to the finish line at the Museum.

We had identifying chips on our shoelaces, and someone had thoughtfully left the electronic pad for us to run across at the Museum, so eventually we got confirmation in the mail that we had indeed finished. Our time: 7:28. A seven and a half hour run, and I was seventy years old. That's 26.2 miles of which the last two-tenths may be the hardest.

Lee

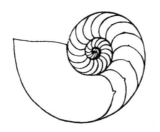

India, Nepal, and Tibet

Lee

Impressions of India

Arriving jet-lagged in India is cultural overload,

is being tumbled in a kaleidoscope,

assaulted by colors,

pounded by sounds,

melted by heat,

*and overwhelmed by a riot of smells: exhaust
fumes, curries, garbage, marigolds, cigarette
smoke, incense, urine, spices, coconut husks.*

I saw lovely dark-haired women climbing ladders

carrying hods of cement while wearing saris.

Pedestrians are challenged by the press of people,

*looming lorries, three-wheeled taxis, buses,
bicycles, autos – and cows.*

They honk, tinkle, blat, growl, put-put, rattle, roar

at a painful decibel level.

Lee

I don't remember "moos,"

but once I saw a dead cow in the street.

In the ashram, respite.

Solemn, bearded "sadhus" with their begging bowls

stand beneath an ancient tree awaiting milk.

There is welcome shade.

And silence.

Silence but for the white-garbed men and boys

chanting prayers in Sanskrit.

And the occasional peacock scream.

On the Everest Trail

Prayer Wheels, Khatas, and Mani Stones

No, I didn't climb Mount Everest. I never intended to climb Mount Everest. My intended destination was Tengboche Monastery at 12,700 feet, and I accomplished that.

Back story: After my extended stay with Susan Baldwin in southern India, I spent a week in Madras with the family of our Indian neighbors in New Jersey. From there it was a long train trip to Calcutta where I rode in a rickshaw drawn by an elderly man. I did not enjoy it, and I did not meet Mother Teresa. Thence another train trip to Darjeeling, which at 6,700 feet, offered relief from the oppressive heat that characterizes most of the sub-continent. In Darjeeling there were tea plantations above the clouds.

I would visit Agra and the Taj Mahal on my return trip to Mumbai.

Lee

A hired car transported me from Darjeeling to the border at Siliguri whence I took an Everest Air flight from Bhadrapur to Katmandu, Nepal. Katmandu! What a wonderful city! It has interesting architecture, and one can enjoy every kind of cuisine there. Practical clothing is available and inexpensive. There are shops that sell all sorts of hiking and climbing equipment. I even found a library where one could exchange pocketbooks for a pittance.

Susan had introduced me to Krishna, the travel agent who made my arrangements to hike the Everest Trail. He helped getting the required permits and chose U Taam to be my sherpa. When we met, U Taam presented me with a sturdy hiking stick with an Om carved on the shaft. It served well. I still have it.

On the trek, U Taam carried my pack and sleeping bag. I kept my water bottle and fanny pack with sunscreen and such handy. Days were fiercely hot, and I wore a long-sleeved white shirt for protection from the sun. At night we would stop at teahouses to eat – whatever was available, then sleep side by side in one big dormitory room on hard benches covered with oriental rugs.

All the villages we passed through had prayer wheels where you enter: some large and elaborate, others as simple as painted lard cans. There are also small portable prayer wheels. Inside each wheel are many tiny papers inscribed with prayers. Spinning the wheels (always clockwise) as one passes by, activates all those prayers.

On the eighth day, I was thrilled to reach Namche Bazaar, the small town that had been Sir Edmond Hillary's base camp. Since the next day's hike to Tengboche Monastery would gain considerable elevation, the guidebook suggested two overnights in Namche with an up-and-back climb on the second day for altitude acclimatization.

On day nine the destination for our acclimatization climb was a monastery whose name I have forgotten. We were within sight of it atop a hill when I told U Taam I thought I had had enough

Lee

for that day and suggested we make the teahouse below the monastery our turn-around point.

As we approached the teahouse we could hear chanting. The hosts ushered us up a ladder to an upper room where six orange-robed lamas had come for a mid-day meal. I didn't have to go to the monastery; the monastery came to me – sort of like the mountain coming to Mohammed.

That extra climb and overnight at Namche Bazaar was sound advice. I never suffered altitude sickness. It also helped that my pace was slow. The three young guys who didn't stop at Namche got so ill they had to abort and return to lower altitude.

Much of the trail to Tengboche was lined with mani stones, standing rock faces, flagstones, or flakes inscribed with the Sanskrit mantra "Om mani padme hum."

(The first word Om is a sacred syllable found in Indian religions. The word Mani means "jewel"- or "bead," Padme meaning the "lotus flower," the Buddhist sacred flower, while Hum represents the spirit of enlightenment. It is commonly carved onto rocks or written on paper which is inserted into prayer wheels.)

Tengboche is surrounded by snow-capped mountains, and it was freezing cold there. I was wearing all my layers in the frigid air when I watched a beautiful two-year-old Nepali boy get his morning bath outdoors!

I acquired a khata, a long, white, prayer shawl, to present to the lama at the monastery. As is customary, he presented me with one.

Next? The Jomsom Trail to Muktinath.

Muktinath: Earth, Air, Fire, Water

After my trek on the Everest Trail with Sherpa U Taam, I returned to Kathmandu where my friend, Keirin joined me for more trekking. From Kathmandu we flew to Pokhara and from Pokhara to Jomsom where we began to hike the Jomsom Trail to Muktinath.

Muktinath is an ancient pilgrimage site in Nepal, at 12,300 feet in the Annapurna Mountain Range. The shrine is sacred to both Hindus and Buddhists. Muktinath is special, perhaps unique, in that it may be the only place where all the elements are found together, earth, air, water, and fire.

The temple at Muktinath is grounded on earth; trees even grow there, despite the altitude. Many pilgrims have walked there barefoot, all the way from southern India.

Altitude and exposure mean there is always wind, so hundreds, maybe thousands of prayer flags are always fluttering in the air.

The Annapurna area is volcanic; therefore, there are many fumaroles, or smoking vents, some of which emit flames. At Muktinath the Earth spouting fire has always had a mystical aura.

There is a sacred spring at Muktinath whose water flows from one hundred eight bull-nose spouts into a rectangular pool. One hundred eight is a sacred number, and the most devout pilgrims stand under each spout for purification.

It was a peaceful, awe-inspiring place.

Instead of continuing on the Jomsom Trail, whose pass is at 15,000 feet, Keirin and I retraced our route, much of it in rain. We did get occasional sightings of Annapurna, the first mountain over 8,000 meters to be climbed. (Annapurna is 26,000 feet, Everest is 29,000.) Keirin and I had ponchos to protect our packs and sleeping bags, but we sweated under them, and we hiked in Teva sandals instead of boots. Puddles, running streams, and muddy trails where horses had been before us, didn't faze the rugged Tevas. They would simply go with us into the shower at the next rest stop.

Descent from Muktinath

I have a photograph
taken high in the Himalaya
of two young, red-robed Buddhist nuns.

They have completed their pilgrimage
to the ancient sacred site
and are playfully dancing their way down.

Anachronistically,
one carries a camera,
the other, a plastic water bottle.

Their joy is so radiant,
they seem almost to float
in that rarified air.

Two smiling, red-robed girls
paint the only spot of color
on a vast, gray, rubbled landscape.

Lhasa

Pilgrims still prostrate themselves
inching around the sacred circuits,
forehead to ground,
body length after body length.
Tiny elders in traditional dark garb and braids
still pray for hours at the Jokhang,
Tibet's most sacred temple
just beyond the boisterous city market.
Sometimes the elders offer sweet, shy smiles
to the staring tourists.
One sees few young Tibetans.

With its thousands of steps,
the massive white and ochre Potala
still rises above – as it has for centuries –
one of the highest cities in the world.
Fortress, palace, residence of the exiled Dalai Lama,
this monumental Buddhist symbol
now seems hollow, sad, expectant,
awaiting his return.

Lee

Just down the street, neon glares
and glitz prevails.
New buildings sport white tile and gleaming glass.
Department and computer stores
flaunt latest wares. Young Chinese women
strut in platform shoes and mini-skirts,
and every other shop's a bar.
One wonders where the lamas are.

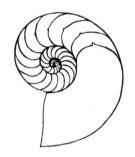

More Miles

Lee

Russia in Winter

Helen Sharpe and I first met in 1951 as members of the Methodist Youth Caravan. I was a Junior at Duke; she was a recent graduate of University of North Carolina at Greensboro as well as a recent bride.

Most of that summer the twelve of us labored in Germany and Austria, shoveling World War II rubble and working with youth groups in both countries. Work accomplished, we enjoyed a Grand Tour: Italy, Switzerland, France, and England.

Helen and I bonded that summer, and we continued to write each other through the years. I would often visit Helen after visiting family in North Carolina.

Exactly thirty years after our Europe trip, Helen wrote to ask if I would like to join her on a trip to Russia with University of North Carolina Russian

Lee

professor and his students studying Russian. Would I!!!

It was still the Cold War Era in 1981, and Intourist monitored the movements of Western tourists closely; nevertheless, many of the young students of Russian did get to visit in some Russian homes.

This was a winter tour, so everything that wasn't plowed was buried in hip-deep snow or frozen. Days were short and nights long. Still we managed to get to a performance of the world-famous Bolshoi Ballet in Moscow and to visit the world-famous Hermitage Museum in St. Petersburg.

Later on the tour we would visit Tiblisi, Georgia where it was warmer, and where there were melons in the market. Tblisi happened to be just a few kilometers east of Batum on the Black Sea where I had been with husband and babes in 1956!

While we were in Moscow, I discovered that a number of the young students were runners. I was then in training for my first marathon, so many mornings, in the winter dark, we would meet before breakfast and jog together. One morning no one seemed to be waiting in the lobby. I couldn't decide if I was too early or too late, so I went on a run by myself, in the snow, in the dark, in the cold, circling around the Kremlin and the colorful spires of St. Basil's. It was magical!

Lee

New Year's Eve, 1981

White flakes fall on Red Square,
dancing, as we dance,
in the crisp night air.
In a swirl of crystal hexagons
we sway in circles on the cobbles,
hugging hefty comrades
crowned in fur.

White flakes fall on Red Square,
frosting St. Basil's
glazing gold domes,
glistening on those glowing faces
(vodka-warm and vodka-rosy)
Gold teeth flash in the greeting we share:
"S NOVOM GODOM!" "Happy New Year!"

White flakes fall on Red Square,
muting the music,
(accordion, balalaika in plaintive air)

muting the clang of the Kremlin clock,
muting the crunch of marching boots
changing the guard at Lenin's tomb
every hour on the hour.

White flakes fall on Red Square,
as, arm in arm, we dance companionably there.
East and West spontaneously embrace,
creating a warmth in that frozen place
while two cold soldiers stand and stare,
stiff and rigid as the arms they bear.

It's a New Year. Would they rather be dancing
(arm in arm, or pair by pair)
with the comrades, with the strangers,
among the still, white, falling snowflakes
on Red Square?

I Was a Spy for TWA

At some point, while I was working for Weez in the ski shop, I was thumbing through a magazine in a doctor or dentist waiting room. And in that magazine was an ad asking the reader if he or she would like a job requiring lots of air travel. Here I admit I committed vandalism: I didn't just make a note of that phone number and address, I tore the page right out of the magazine.

Nor did it take me long to write to TWA inquiring about the opportunity. And it didn't take long to get a letter back saying they had a full component at the time but "they would keep my letter on file." Well, I thought, "That's the end of that!"

Imagine my surprise when maybe half a year later I got a letter from TWA asking if I were still interested. After my enthusiastic YES, I was invited to fly to St. Louis, (tickets enclosed) to see if they liked me and I liked them. Twelve of us were selected, and what a diverse group we were! There was an elderly retired woman who had been a nurse/stewardess for Pan Am, a simple farm wife from the Midwest, a young man who sold perfume in an upscale department store, a sophisticated middle-aged New York woman, a gay theater critic, an obviously ex-military older guy, and a blond bombshell from Palm Beach. Clearly TWA was seeking a cross-section of the population.

Before my yes, TWA had made it clear that this would *not* be a paying position. I would be an incognito Quality Control person responsible for evaluating every aspect of airline service in exchange for getting to fly all over the place.

Weez was lenient and allowed me a flexible ski shop schedule. So every month the Quality Control group flew to St. Louis for a meeting where we stayed overnight in a posh hotel near the waterfront. (As I was in training for a marathon, my early morning run would usually include circling the Gateway Arch.) Every month TWA provided three sets of destinations to be visited which we rated preferentially. Usually we got our first choice of the lists.

My departure/return airport was always Newark, but often I would have to go through St. Louis on my way to an assigned destination. Meals and lodging were reimbursed on our overnights. European destinations required at least two overnights. If we wanted to stay longer in some city to play tourist or visit friends, that was fine – as long as we got to all the destinations on our list during the month.

Being a Quality Control person was not easy; it required lots of work. We had to make reservations and evaluate the ticket agents. No drinking or sleeping on flights as we had to observe the flight attendants and report any rudeness or lack of attention. On arrivals we had to observe and evaluate airport agent services as well as baggage claim efficiency. Completing all those check lists consumed many hours.

But for eighteen months I got to fly to at least four different places every month, often staying a week visiting friends or touring cities and localities new to me. We were supposed to fly coach, but often we would get upgraded because we flew so much. (Upgrades were allowed; it would have seemed strange and suspicious to say, "I'd really rather fly coach." So sometimes we flew first class.)

Several trips were to Europe: Brussels, Paris, Copenhagen, and one to Rome – after which I got to spend time in Naples with the DeMartino family who had been our neighbors and best friends when we lived in Italy.

Alas, if Quality Control people worked longer than eighteen months, we would likely get recognized and identified as spies. Anyway, sadly, TWA is no more.

Travels with Nan

Nancy Strickland and I met on a cross-country ski trip some time in the 90's. We had each signed up as a single looking for a roommate, and Joanne Hartnet, the trip leader put us together, saying "I think you'll like each other." The rest is – as they say – history.

We did indeed hit it off and agreed to be roommates on future trips, sometimes to Lake Placid, or Lapland Lake in New York, more often to Stowe, Vermont where we skied at the Trapp Family Lodge. Saturday mornings we would huff and puff the long way up to the cabin and pause for soup before the long ski down, then ski easier runs in the afternoon. As we grew older and less energetic we would still dutifully trudge up to the cabin in the morning, but afternoons were more often spent in the Russian Tea Room than on the slopes.

Before I knew her, Nan and her husband Jim had made some fabulous trips with West Point graduates. They had toured Russia and done the China Gorge trip before the dams inundated so much. When Jim decided he had done enough, Nan wasn't nearly done traveling, so she and I became travel buddies.

Soon after I moved from Pennsylvania to Arizona, Nan came to visit. At that time I was living with daughter Lisa and her husband Pat. Locally, Nan and I went birding at Mary Jo's B n B, hiked a bit up Ramsey Canyon, and admired hummingbirds at the Nature Center. Did we visit the Kartchner Caverns? Perhaps.

Then we went on a big circle tour of **Arizona and New Mexico.** I drove; Nan navigated. We visited my brother Bill in Prescott whence the three of us took the fabled Verde Canyon train trip. Although we didn't see the promised eagles, we were glad Nan had suggested that delightful excursion.

My brother Bill escorted us to artsy mining town Jerome, and to Sedona of the red rocks and world-famous vortex.

Lee

On our own Nan and I were in time for the first early morning tour of Meteor Crater where the astronauts train. Thence through the colorful Painted Desert.

In preparation for this tour of Indian territory I had re-read all the Tony Hillerman novels and was hoping to see Shiprock. Alas, we had neglected to remember that the Navajo Nation is on daylight time while the rest of Arizona is not, so we had to bypass Shiprock in order to arrive on time at Chinle and our scheduled Elder Hostel tour of **Canyon de Chelly**.

Canyon de Chelly. What a marvel! Do Google this special place to see some of the wonders we got to see up close. In 2006, I was recovering from radiation and chemotherapy, so, was pleased and proud that I managed the hike down to the valley and back up. Nan gifted me with a handsome blue-white-black square pot whose young creator I met and spoke with in the valley. The pot's designs echo those ancient drawings by the cave dwellings.

X X X

At some point I asked well-traveled Lisa and Pat about their favorite destination and they chorused "Tikal!" Thus Nan's and my next trip was to **Guatemala**. Those grey stone pyramids rising out of the jungle are spectacular – and steep to climb! At one of the many museum's gift shops Nan bought me my favorite colorful woven scarf. Did I mention that Nan is generous?

X X X

In November of 2008, just after Mr. Obama's election as President, Nan and I went with Odysseys Unlimited to **Kenya**. We were almost mobbed by thrilled Kenyan young people who coveted our Obama buttons. How can one begin to describe Kenya? Marvelous as photographs are, they pale beside up-close looks at elephants, rhinos, wildebeests, spear-wielding jumpers, hippos, giraffes, warthogs, exotic birds, iconic acacia trees. One morning from our jeep we watched a mother cheetah and her two kits chase down and kill a small deer. The deed was over in seconds, but the mother cheetah had to keep charging a threatening

Lee

hyena while the young cheetahs feasted. We got good looks at Mt. Kilimanjaro and stood in two hemispheres at the equator. We also visited a Maasai village, home to those remarkable, tall, slender, spear-weilding jumpers I first encountered in the movie *King Solomon's Mines.*

X X X

The last trip Nan and I made together was in 2011. (It was most likely my last big trip.) Odysseys again took us to **Peru, The Galapagos**, and **Ecuador**. Our visit to **Machu Picchu** was my third. (Along with Venice, it is one of my favorite places on the panet.) Cuzco and The Sacred Valley were also repeats for me, but not the famous Galapagos Islands where aboard the Motor Yacht *Coral II*, by rubber dinghy, or on foot we saw huge iguanas, colorful crabs, roaring sea lions, giant tortoises, tiny penguins, and – my favorite – blue-footed boobies. And of course Darwin's famous finches.

Back in Quito we watched the Cotopaxi volcano spewing smoke. And a visit to the Ecological Park finally afforded me a look at Andean condors, the largest of all flying birds with a wingspan of ten feet, birds who can soar to over three miles.

Nan and I were perfect travel companions and roommates. I like to rise early; she prefers to sleep in when she can. Nan usually deferred to me when choices were to be made and she was always accommodating. Though we now live a continent apart, Nan in Pennsylvania, I in Arizona, we stay in close touch by email. I wonder if we'll travel together again.

Lee

Westward Ho!

How I came to live in Arizona is a convoluted story.

In 2000, I bought a house in Abington, Pennsylvania, to be near my younger daughter, son-in-law, and my two grandchildren. Not long afterward, Hillary, Gray, Daniel, and Susan moved to Germany!

At the time, Lisa and Pat were living in Plantation, Florida, near Fort Lauderdale where Lisa was working for Air France. Pat was an entomologist inspector at Port Everglades. After Lisa had a horrible fall on their kitchen terrazzo floor, Pat decreed she would have to start using a wheelchair; her ataxia had become hazardous to her health.

That decision meant that Pat would have to drive Lisa to work, drive to the Port for his nine to five, then pick up Lisa after work, drive home – by which point neither of them was in the mood to prepare a meal.

Recently, but before Lisa's fall, I had had an enjoyable stay with them in Plantation. That visit may have been what prompted Pat to ask Lisa, "Why don't you ask your mother to come live with us?"

As I no longer had any compelling reason to remain in Abington, I said yes.

After Herb left New Jersey, where he had lived briefly with each daughter, he settled in Roanoke, Virginia. A minor automobile accident, plus his ataxia, caused him to lose his driver's license, and in losing his license Herb lost his mobility and his independence. So he asked if he could come to Florida, too.

Well, there was no way the Plantation house could accommodate three households. Several scenarios were proposed: Herb would buy the house next door; Herb would build a house on a nearby lot. Eventually Lisa and Pat decided they should just retire early. That way there would be just three moves instead of five.

Lee

As long as Lisa worked for Air France, she was the primary breadwinner. Those travel benefits took precedence. However, their agreement was that when it was time to retire, Pat would get to choose. For Pat it was a no-brainer; he and Lisa would live in southeastern Arizona. As an entomologist Pat was aware that southeast Arizona has the most variety of flora and fauna of any state in the contiguous forty-eight. In fact he had been coming from California to Arizona to "hunt" since he was young.

I sold my wonderful little house in Abington and headed south to North Carolina where I visited Ruth Ledford, my friend since childhood, and Helen Sharpe, a fellow caravaner and travel companion to Russia.

Then I collected Herb in Roanoke and we headed west to Arizona.

Meanwhile, Lisa and Pat had found a big single-level house on Bannock Avenue in Sierra Vista with a swimming pool and a spectacular view of the Huachucas. There would be a suite on one end for Herb, a suite on the other for me, with Lisa and Pat in the middle. I became chief cook and bottlewasher.

The arrangement worked pretty well, except that Herb was not a happy camper. The loss of his independence and mobility was killing him – literally. He stuck it out for a nine months "gestation" period before he killed himself.

When a four-acre property near the Ramsey Canyon Nature Center became available, Lisa and Pat eagerly purchased it. As their new place is almost 1,000 feet higher in elevation, insect-hunting in "Oaks" is even better than in Bannock's "high desert."

When they moved, so did I. My new home is in Mountain View Gardens "Gracious Retirement Living." I share my apartment with my cat, Bouquet, and enjoy a spectacular view of the Huachucas from my third-floor apartment.

Lee

To Spain with Lisa

While living Italy, Lisa and I made a trip to Spain on one of her Spring Breaks. On our way we drove through Monaco and thought of Grace Kelly. In southern France we made a point to go to Nimes to see the picturesque Pont du Gard. Despite its name, it's not a bridge but an ancient Roman aqueduct. Over and over we sang the 15th century folk song:

> *Sur le Pont d'Avignon*
> *On y danse, On y danse*
> *Sur le Pont d'Avignon*
> *On y danse tous en rond.*

We passed through Andorra on our way to Barcelona, our first stop in Spain. In Barcelona we enjoyed a visit to the Picasso Museum featuring the artist's formative work. We stood in awe before Gaudi's gaudy, modernist cathedral, La Sagrada Familia.

Thence inland to Madrid. Much of our time in Madrid was spent in the Museo Nacional del Prado, Spain's most famous Art Museum. Somehow we bypassed Don Quixote's iconic windmills.

We happened to arrive in Seville at the most auspicious time. Feria De Abril De Sevilla begins two weeks after Holy Week, and for those six days Seville doesn't sleep. There is a marvelous horseback parade with traditional costumes in which the women's ruffled gowns drape over the horses' haunches. And there is much visiting between *casetas* with ceremonial drinking of sherry.

When you returned to your hotel after late *tapas* and even later dinner, it was necessary to clap loudly to summon the night watchman who would let you in with a gigantic key. Most memorable to me was how in the dark someone would begin clapping softly. Soon others would join in, and a veritable orchestra of syncopated clapping would follow. Magical.

We went to Granada especially to visit The Alhambra, the ornate Moorish palace and fortress.

Lee

Our hotel close by was a Parador, this one formerly a convent. (Paradores are a network of over 90 state-run Spanish hotels consisting of restored Castles, Monasteries, Convents, Fortresses, Manor Houses and Palaces.) Our dining room was a refectory so long it seemed endless.

The morning we were to leave, the now famous tan VW had a flat. Two "gentlemen" sat on the veranda and watched me change the tire. Thanks to Herb's training I had no trouble.

Before heading back to Naples, we crossed the Strait of Gibraltar to Morocco. (We must have seen the Rock if not its infamous monkeys.) Morocco was exotic and colorful. In one of the bazaars Lisa bargained with the shopkeeper for a lovely, shallow, dark, shaped-by-hand wooden salad bowl. She was much better at bargaining than I was, and the vendors where charmed by her. I wonder where that salad bowl is now.

Italy Revisited with Hillary

In June of 2013, violinists Daniel and Susan went on tour with Stretto, their Princeton-based chamber orchestra. (On an earlier tour I had accompanied them to Florence, Split, Dubrovnik, and Prague.) Hillary accompanied them on the 2013 tour where they played concerts in Brussels, Villach, Belgrade, and Sofia.

Earlier, Hillary had asked me if I wanted to meet her when the orchestra tour was over to make a nostalgia trip to Italy. My response was an enthusiastic Yes! So, Hillary left the tour and the kids at Sofia, Bulgaria, and flew to Rome where she met me.

Our three days in Rome were full. We spent a long time in the Vatican admiring Michelangelo's frescoes in the Sistine Chapel. We walked a lot and enjoyed all the hop-on, hop-off bus tours which took us to the Colosseum, the Roman Forum, St. Peter's, the Trevi Fountain and the Seven Hills. The scenes

Lee

reminded me of Resphigi's *Pines of Rome* and *Fountains of Rome.*

Next, we took the train south to Naples. This visit was the most nostalgic as we had lived in a suburb of Napoli for five years in the 60's. Our mission in Naples was to eat pizza in all the best pizzerias. Hillary had done the research on-line. We did most of our gift-shopping in colorful, crowded Neapolitan markets where bargaining is mandatory. Naples had hop-on, hop-off buses also. As we preferred the upper deck – so as to see more – Hillary bought from the port-side vendor, great, wide-brimmed straw hats to shade us from the hot sun. The tour that ran along the coast took us almost but not quite to Pozzuoli where we had lived.

After Naples there was a long train trip north to Florence. One of our main objectives was to see Michelangelo's *David* in the Academia. We knew we would need reservations, so that was the first thing we checked out in the tourist office near the train station. We followed the directions and found ourselves in a long line that moved ever so slowly in the hot sun. But it wasn't a line for tickets; it was a line to get into the Academia! We were able to stay as long as we liked, gazing at the *David* from every viewpoint.

While traveling with one of the orchestra tours, Hillary and I made a mad dash to see one of our favorite pieces of art, Fra Angelico's fresco of *The Annunciation* in the Convent of San Marco – only to find the convent closed. It was high on our list for Florence, and this time we were successful.

Florence also had hop-on, hop-off bus tours that gave us access to the world famous Uffizi art museum, housing Brunelleschi Duomo, the famous doors of the Baptistry, and the Ponte Vecchio with its shops lining the bridge over the Arno.

From Florence we took the night train to Venice, possibly the favorite city of both Hillary and me. No bus tour here! No land vehicles. Even a bicycle would be inconvenient. The only public transportation is on the water by one of the many vaporetti that ply the canals. Or by gondola, which is much too expensive to do more than once. Mostly people walk as Venice isn't all that large. Walking means climbing up an arched bridge over a canal then descending on the other side every block or so. Picture the famous one, the Rialto.

Venice's cathedral is perhaps the easiest to appreciate anywhere, as it faces the huge Piazza San Marco where one may take a meal or a coffee and gaze at its splendor at leisure. I am particularly fond of the great bronze horses above the basilica.

The two-mile-long Grand Canal has been described as "the finest street in all the world and has the finest houses." One of those fine palazzos houses the superb Peggy Guggenheim modern art collection which we visited for the second time.

We did not visit the famous blown glass factory at Murano this trip, but we did make more than one excursion to the Lido where Hillary swam and I people-watched.

Our trip to the Venice airport involved a long vaporetto ride on the water. Can you smell the salty air?

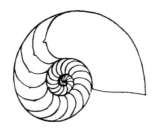

Letting Go

Lee

The Day My Father Died

It happened on the sixth of April in 1971. Daddy was seventy-four years old. He had been a heavy smoker all his life, but he didn't die of lung cancer. It was some virulent, fast-growing cancer that quickly invaded all his organs.

I was living in Italy when I got the telephone call from Mother saying I should probably come home now. Although we were civilians, Herb was working for the US Sixth Fleet in Naples, and the Navy offered me Compassionate military transportation to the States.

That sounds simple but few things are that easy. Herb's parting advice to me was "Take anything that moves." So my first flight was to Düsseldorf, then one to a US air base in England (Mildenhall? Lakenheath?), and finally a flight to McGuire AFB in New Jersey whence I could take a train to North Carolina.

Military planes are not built for passenger comfort; hard seating is on benches the length of

Lee

the fuselage. (There *are* seat belts.) One set of
pilots, knowing I was on Compassionate Leave,
invited me into the cockpit and gave me earphones
so I could hear the communications. I loved it.

It must have taken me fifteen hours or more to
get from Naples to North Carolina, but when I
arrived, Daddy was still alive – though heavily
sedated. On the chance that he could hear me, I
said, "Daddy, it's Pam. I've come a long way to see
you." And to our amazement, he answered, "Bless
you, Pam." Naturally, I wept.

Mother and Aunt Mabel, Daddy's older sister,
noticed I was drooping and suggested I lie down in
the waiting room down the hall. I did and had a
refreshing nap. When I returned to Daddy's room,
Mother looked tired and drowsy, so Aunt Mabel and I
persuaded her to lie down in that same waiting
room. Before she would go, she made us promise to
call her if there was any change.

Well, wouldn't you know; she probably hadn't
been gone five minutes when Daddy did rouse. I
quickly ran down the hall only to find Mother in a

deep sleep. Promise or no promise, I didn't have the heart to wake her, just returned to Daddy's room to see if he really was rousing. He wasn't.

Three or four minutes later Mother appeared. "What did Hix want?" she queried. Aunt Mabel and I shrugged and told her he hadn't said anything. Mother insisted, "Yes he did. He called me." And within minutes he died.

What struck me when the orderlies came to zip him in the dark gray bag was how small he looked, he who had always seemed larger than life.

By now it was beginning to get light. Daddy had been in Duke Hospital, so from the hospital Mother and I walked down to the Sarah P. Duke Memorial Gardens. The family had enjoyed many happy hours there through the years.

It was April; the piney woods were full of yellow daffodills, the formal terraces laced with Spring bloomers. New life was burgeoning. It happened to be Palm Sunday.

It's Okay, Mother

Mother was ninety years old when she died in 2004. The last two years of her life she had senile dementia but not Alzheimer's according to Duke Hospital.

Mother never failed to recognize my brother Bill and me, and she was always clearly glad to see us. She was delighted with great-grandson, Daniel, as a baby, as a one-year-old, and as a two-year-old. She did get repetitive and several times asked Hillary's husband, Gray, "Is this your first trip to North Carolina?"

In those last two years when Bill and I would visit – separately or together – each of us would tell her it was all right with us if she wanted to move on. "Mother, you've done a good job. Bill and I are fine. It's okay if you decide to leave us."

Allow me to back up a bit. Bill and Lorinda were getting divorced, and the process was looking to be acrimonious. Both worked for Ma Bell, or AT&T

– Bill as an engineer, Lorinda as a mathematics whiz. He happily helped her with dog shows and her car racing. She, on the other hand, would not go sailing with him or accompany him to his curling events. Bill, on the phone to me: "She wants the vintage Datsun and all three dogs..." (They raised Dobermanns.) I interrupted: "Bill, Bill, get yourself in the EST program; this doesn't have to be ugly. You can have a civilized divorce in which both you and Lorinda will be satisfied; you can part amicably if you'll just take the Training."

I was referring the the Werner Earhart Seminar Training to which Hillary introduced me, the family, and numerous friends. Bill had been a guest at EST seminars so he knew what I was talking about. Apparently he heard me, as he signed up for the next available EST week-end.

It worked as I had promised. And Bill was so impressed with the Training's effectiveness, he began signing up for extra seminars such as "It's About Time" and "Be Here Now."

Lee

During one seminar, when he was a volunteer, he spotted a woman who really interested him. Privy to registration information, he obtained her telephone number and invited her to go with him to a curling match in which he was competing. She said yes, and the rest, as they say, was history.

Susan Baldwin had come to EST looking for help with her grief over her eighteen-year-old daughter's death. Susan had been a full partner with her architect husband in a successful architectural firm. After their daughter's death, they divorced, and Susan became a wealthy woman in the settlement.

Bill had already moved in with her when Susan decided they should take a trip around the world, concentrating on third world countries and spiritual places. They had an audience with Mother Theresa, for example.

Susan and Bill continued searching. They had been doing a series of Jaffe workshops, the latest one in Italy. This particular workshop had to do with death and dying. Participants were to write a will

388

and compose letters to people with whom they needed closure or forgiveness.

One of the Jaffe exercises involved simulating death. This exercise must absolutely be done with an observant partner because it is possible to go too deep in the process. (Many people in India choose to die in such a way.)

It was Susan's turn to simulate death. She had reclined, relaxed and was breathing slowly when she suddenly sat up and exclaimed, "Bill, Bill, let's take your mother with us!"

The very next morning they got my phone call. Mother had died that night.

Lee

I Miss You, Bill

I was on my way home from Kenya when my brother Bill became moribund. It had to have been in November of 2008, because the Odysseys tour that Nancy Strickland and I enjoyed had arrived in Nairobi mere days after Barack Obama was elected President. Not surprisingly, the Kenyans were ecstatic; everyone coveted the Obama pin on my fanny pack.

Bill was in hospice care in Prescott, Arizona when I arrived, jet lagged after flights from Africa to Philadelphia and from Philadelphia to Phoenix. He was heavily sedated, but I am confident he was aware of my presence. Bill's son, Bob, and Bob's wife, Alice, were at his bedside as were my daughter, Lisa, and her husband, Pat. The five of us talked to Bill and stroked him during those last days of his life, and got better acquainted with each other over evening dinners together. The folks at the hospice facility could not have been kinder to Bill or to us.

Bill, my only sibling, was five years younger than me. As kids we fought and were pretty evenly matched. As adults we grew fond of each other and were as close as siblings can be who live half a world apart. After graduating from Duke as an engineer, Bill did two tours with Westinghouse in Kwajalein in the Pacific while I was living in the Middle East or Italy.

When we would get together, my young daughters Lisa and Hillary would squeal, "Unca BEE-o! Unca BEE-o!" Clearly, they adored him.

Physical problems plagued Bill much of his life. He had had surgery for stomach ulcers before he finished university, and in his later years he developed terrible psoriasis which contributed to his death.

Bill had experienced heartache. Gail, his first wife, left him for a man she met on Kwaj and took the two young boys, Bob and Charles, with her. And Bill and his second wife, Lorinda, divorced.

Lee

Bill met Susan Baldwin at an EST seminar, and they became a pair. They enjoyed many travels and seminars together – some of which Susan invited me on. Later, Susan began living in India six months of the year as a devotee, first to Sai Baba, later to a different guru. It was Susan who made my trip to India possible.

After Bill and I both retired in Arizona, he in Prescott, I in Sierra Vista, we visited each other often. Even when we weren't physically together, we would talk on the phone, especially during Duke basketball games. That's what I miss most.

My favorite remark about my brother? Once, when Bill arrived at a spiritual course Susan was taking, a woman who did not know of Bill's connection with Susan, exclaimed, "Oh look at that beautiful pink heart!" She was able to see my brother's aura.

Not My Best Year

In the summer of 2005, Herb and I moved to Arizona – from Virginia and Pennsylvania, respectively – to live with Lisa and Pat in Sierra Vista.

In December, I was diagnosed with anal cancer. Thus 2006 began under a black cloud.

Six weeks of radiation sessions and oral chemotherapy began in January and concluded in February. The chemo made me so weak I needed Pat's assistance to get to my Monday through Friday radiation sessions. The radiation burns were extremely painful.

The chemo left me so debilitated I could hardly move; the inactivity caused a deep vein thrombosis which landed me in the hospital – and put me on coumadin for the rest of my life. It was my second DVT.

My hearing had begun to go south. In March the local Eye Ear Nose and Throat doctor suspected an acoustic neuroma. He referred me to Phoenix where Dr. Daspit confirmed the diagnosis. Acoustic neuromas are almost never malignant, but they need to be arrested lest they impinge on the auditory or facial nerve. Dr. Daspit, one of the few doctors who performed gamma knife surgery, scheduled me for the procedure in April. I would be the subject for his teaching the technique.

Pat and Lisa took me to Phoenix where I stayed overnight with Susan Stoner, who took me to the early morning surgical date. Several EENT residents observed the procedures. Three holes were drilled in my head to secure the clamp that would hold my head steady while it was being bombarded with gamma rays. Thorough mapping of the neuroma had been done beforehand to ensure the radiation avoided facial and auditory nerves.

Much more than you wanted to know, right?

And there's more. After the surgery on April 6, Pat, Lisa and I returned to Sierra Vista, and Pat ordered pizza with all the works for our supper. When I went to summon Herb, I knew something was wrong and didn't enter his apartment. Instead, I called Pat who confirmed that Herb had killed himself.

Did the cancer cause me to lose my hair? Not on my head – just my pubic hair. The good news is that I have now been cancer-free for ten years.

Lee

Contemplations on Loss

At our age, and living as we do among mostly elderly retired people, one must expect to lose people more frequently than the typical population. But it still hurts.

How we miss Phil who needed more care and has moved just down the highway to the Beehive. The empty space at the table where he used to sit seems like a black hole.

And dear, sweet Donna, briefly ill and then *really* gone. (Helen hopes she is hearing beautiful music. Don't we all.) Notice how often a bereaved person doesn't long survive the loss of a spouse.

What I noticed after Herb died – ten years ago now – was how often I thought of things I wanted to tell him, only to realize that I no longer could.

During our fifty-three years of marriage Herb's work as an engineer often took him away from home base – wherever *that* was – for long periods of time, sometimes on sea trials, sometimes to far off assignments where families were not welcome. I became accustomed to his occasional absences, prompting me to write this:

While You Were Away

Monday it rained. Monsoons already?

Sudden thunder scared the cat (and me)

Right out of our chair!

It must have been that same lightning strike

That fried the phone.

The Qwest man says the problem's mine,

Not theirs. Unfair!

The baby quail can fly now.

I watched them crossing Cherokee,

Running like over-wound wind-up toys on wheels,

Then, suddenly! into the air.

Lee

Cara Mia had a flat.

Can you believe?

The Triple A man couldn't remove the tire

And had to tow her in for repair!

The rosemary's doing well,

Has reached the wall – just barely.

How long before it cascades?

(My hair grows faster.)

Oh dear. Cinco caught a baby bunny

And left it by my door.

Spare me such gifts.

One day the wind went on a tear

And blew the emptied trash container

Clear across the street and into Millers' yard.

Hey! The space station passed overhead

While you were away –

Bright as any star.

I'm sorry you missed it.

But I'm aware:

This time you won't be coming back.

Lee

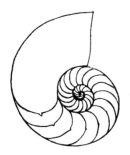

Theater I've Loved

Lee

My First Musical

The first musical I ever saw was *Oklahoma!* I was sixteen, in New York City with the Columbia Scholastic Press Association. My big brother Shin, a Duke pre-med student, was in Manhattan visiting his parents Kimi and Isawo Tanaka. (Isawo and my father were students together at Trinity College before it became Duke University.) So the Tanakas invited me to dinner, and afterward Shin gave me a gardenia corsage and took me to see *Oklahoma!*

So began my love of the medium. Perhaps my all-time favorite is *The Music Man*, but all have been in their way magical: *Candide, The Fantasticks, Man of La Mancha, Evita, Sweeny Todd, South Pacific, A Little Night Music, Pippin, Guys and Dolls, Fiddler on the Roof....*

Show tunes frequently surface; something will trigger a memory, an association, and I'll find myself humming along. It could be "I'm Gonna Wash That Man Right Outa My Hair," or "I Got the Horse Right

Lee

Here," or "Don't Cry for Me, Argentina," or "If I Were a Rich Man," or "To Dream the Impossible Dream." And I smile.

Theater I've Loved, Part I

I've always loved theater – ever since I got to be Spring in fourth grade. In high school I was Elizabeth Bennet in *Pride and Prejudice.* At Duke I played Maria in Shakespeare's *Twelfth Night* and Raina's mother in Shaw's *Arms and the Man.* In my long life I have been fortunate to see many great lights of the theater:

In 1951, I saw Vivien Leigh and Laurence Olivier perform Shakespeare's *Antony and Cleopatra* on a revolving stage in London. (I think my student ticket cost the equivalent of thirty-five cents.)

In 1951, I also saw Agatha Christie's *The Mousetrap*, the longest running play ever. (It is still going!) That summer I also attended the Oberammergau Passion Play, performed every ten years since 1634, as the village's thanks for being spared the Bubonic Plague. Twenty years later I saw both *The Mousetrap* and *The Passion Play* again – this time with my mother.

Lee

Leonard Bernstein and the New York Philharmonic Orchestra came to Duke while I was a student. So did all the world-famous string quartets. Small group ensembles loved the acoustics of the small theater in East Duke, one of the oldest buildings on the original campus.

One big thrill was seeing Alec Guinness, one of my favorite actors, portraying Dylan Thomas. The play, called *Dylan*, and Sir Alec both won Tonys in 1964.

Once I saw and heard Leontyne Price as Donna Elvira in Mozart's *Don Giovanni* at the Old Met on 39th Street. (It was famous for its superb acoustics. It closed in 1966.)

While I was living in Manhattan my favorite musical was *Candide*, Leonard Bernstein's operetta based on Voltaire's satire by the same name. The music was marvelous, but the best part was how a number of cast members sprang out of the audience in the small theater. Whenever anyone visited, we would go see *Candide*. I think I saw it five times.

Julie Harris won a Tony in 1976 for her performance as the poet Emily Dickinson in *The*

Belle of Amherst, a one-woman two-act play. I think I saw that twice.

Remember Robert Preston? You know him as Professor Harold Hill in *The Music Man*. I saw him in 1976 in *Sly Fox*, an adaptation of Ben Jonson's comedy *Volpone*.

The Judas Kiss is about the later years of Oscar Wilde's life. Liam Neeson played the poet-playright in 1998, a poignant performance.

Polly Pen, a friend of Lisa's and a member of our book club while Lisa and I lived in New Jersey is a prize-winning actress, composer, lyricist. I've seen Polly's *The Night Governess*, *Bed and Sofa*, and *Goblin Market*.

When my daughter Hillary was just two weeks old, I flew with her from North Carolina to New York just to see *The Fourth Son* by Aldyth Morris at NYC's Phoenix Theater. Aldyth had read parts of that play to us as a work in progress when we sat at her feet in Honolulu. Aldyth is better known for *Damien*, her one-man play about Father Damien, the leper priest of Molokai, which had a long run on PBS.

Theater I've Loved, Part II
or How I Once Spent the Night in Central Park

I was living in Abington, Pennsylvania, when I saw a notice about an up-coming play at the Delacorte. The Delacorte is the open air theater in Manhattan's Central Park where every summer there is a series of performances called Shakespeare in the Park. The plays are not always Shakespeare, but it is always top-notch theater, and it is FREE.

Of the many friends I invited to go with me, no one seemed available. Finally, I called Sarah Rivera, one of daughter Hillary's friends. Sarah not only was interested, she was willing to drive into the city.

So off we went to the Big Apple, found a parking spot not too far from the Delacorte, and settled down in the Park to wait in line. Mimes, and madrigalists, jugglers and dancers passed by entertaining those of us waiting. By mid-afternoon Delacorte staff members have counted those in line – allowing two tickets each – and have said to those just ahead of us, "You'll get in." To Sarah and me, "Not tonight."

What to do? We could leave and come back the next day, maybe to have the same abominable luck as today. Or we could stay and keep our now early place in line for the following night's show. We elected to stay. Between us we had one space blanket and lots of good snacks. Sarah moved the car to a more reasonable parking place, and we settled in for the evening.

Actually, no one is allowed to spend the night in Central Park, so at midnight, precisely, New York's finest come in and lead those waiting out onto Fifth Avenue to resettle on the paving stones. No one breaks ranks. Everyone knows who was before and after them. Of course there wasn't much sleep in the City that Never Sleeps, but some folks were playing chess, others cards, some ordering pizza, and the night passed. And at six o'clock, precisely, the police escorted us back into the Park to the very places we had vacated six hours earlier.

Lee

Now for another day's wait. Sarah and I took turns going to the bathroom – and acquiring more food and drink – at a nearby restaurant. I think I had a book. (I had learned never to go anywhere without a book.) One o'clock eventually rolled around, and the staff assured us we were in for that evening. Since we had two tickets each, I invited two New York friends, Polly Pen, the aforementioned playwright-musician, and Susan Blommart, a professional actress (Susan played the nervous secretary in *Guarding Tess*) to join us.

Thus Polly, Susan, Sarah and I got to see Chekhov's *The Seagull* with a cast that included Meryl Streep, Kevin Kline, Philip Seymour Hoffman, Natalie Portman, Christopher Walken, Marcia Gay Harden, John Goodman and several others! Mike Nichols was the director.

Okay. So I didn't exactly spend the night in Central Park. But nearly.

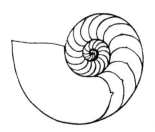

Reading, Writing, Arithmetic

Lee

Writing

Forget Arithmetic. I'm much better at words than numbers. Words have always fascinated me, and from an early age I wanted to combine them into something approaching poetry.

The December after Pearl Harbor, when I was eleven, my Christmas gift to my parents was a poem I wrote called "In This War-torn World." At first my father was fearful I had plagiarized it. When he was convinced it was my original effort, he submitted it to *The North Carolina Christian Advocate*, and they published it. My first time in print.

I continued to dabble in verse throughout my life, and in 2002 – in time for my fiftieth reunion at Duke – I self-published some of the pieces I had accumulated over the years. The resulting "slim, small volume" was entitled *Vultures, Mold, and Other Delights.*

Book Clubs

Until recently, I belonged to two book clubs. Nancy Williams, an excellent and knowledgeable moderator, chairs the one at the Sierra Vista library. My problem is that the library book club has grown to an unwieldy size – sometimes twenty or more participants. The size makes it difficult for everyone to have a say and those who do speak often speak so softly that I can't hear much of what is being said. So I have stopped going.

I particularly liked that third Wednesdays at the library could be all-day affairs: morning discussion of the book, a brown-bag lunch, followed by a filmed version of the book in the afternoon. I'll miss that.

BOOKIES, the other book club, was initiated by my daughter Lisa. Lisa has *always* needed to belong to a book club. As she is now wheel-chair-bound, I did most of the recruiting for our group in Sierra Vista; thus, of the present nine members, seven are

Unitarian Universalists, one I knew from a meditation group, and Lisa who is unaffiliated.

Members take turns meeting in each others' homes. When it is my turn as hostess/Queen, we meet in Mountain View Garden's special dining room. Often we dress in costumes or attire that reflects the work we just read. All of us are food-oriented, and most of us are exceptionally good cooks, so we share a pot-luck meal before the book discussion. When possible, the meal echoes the cuisine of the book. For instance, we enjoyed Indian food before *A Passage to India*, and *Shantaram*, Asian dishes before *Memoirs of a Geisha*, German food for *The Book Thief*, New England fare for *Olive Kitteridge*, and French cuisine with *All the Light We Cannot See*.

For sure, the most memorable book club session ever was not a mere evening but a whole week-end devoted to Emily Dickinson. It was at a time when Lisa and I both happened to be living in New Jersey. A number of the members lived in New York City – among them Polly Pen, herself a poet, musician, and actor, three of whose musicals have been produced.

The group traveled by car to Amherst, Massachusetts where we stayed overnight. The next day we visited Dickinson's home, stood in awed silence in the second-story room where she wrote her poetry at a small desk before a window. Of her 1,800 poems very few were published during her lifetime. Because Miss Emily always wore white, our members also dressed in white the whole week-end.

We had brought with us the makings for dishes of typical New England fare. I'm sure there were baked beans, maybe cod; I remember baking fruit tarts.

Lisa, who was Regent for this event, assigned each of us a particular poem she wanted read aloud and analyzed, another poem of our choice to memorize and recite. We did the readings and explications *al fresco* in the garden of the house where we were staying.

Sunday morning we seated ourselves on the grass around the iron fence surrounding Emily's grave site. That's where we recited the poems we had chosen to memorize. My choice was "Essential Oils."

Play Reading

Some years ago, when BOOKIES was meeting at Lisa's, we had been reading and discussing the poetry of Blake. I quoted a poem of Tennyson's which reminded me of Blake:

Flower in the Crannied wall
I pluck you out of the crannies,
I hold you here, root and all, in my hand,
Little flower – but if I could understand
What you are, root and all, and all in all,
I should know what God and man is.

And THAT, I said, reminded me of some lines from Christopher Fry's verse play, *The Lady's Not for Burning:*

...I can pass to you
Generations of roses in this wrinkled berry.
There: now you hold in your hand a race

of summer gardens....

At which point I remarked that I had always wanted to participate in a reading of that play. Patricia said, "Let's do it!" So we did.

The six BOOKIES all took parts, and we fledged out the eleven characters with Unitarians. Professional actress Jesse St. John played Jennet Jourdemayne to my Thomas Mendip. We did just one reading in the chapel at Mountain View Gardens. Our then minister Rod Richards attended and was quite impressed.

That was such fun we next did Oscar Wilde's *The Importance of Being Earnest.* What a delight.

Then Patricia and Lisa suggested we do Tom Stoppard's *Travesties*, a brilliant *tour de force* which incorporates real historical people as well as characters named Gwendolyn and Cecily in homage to the Wilde play.

I think it was in December of 2013 that I made my directorial debut with a reading of *It's a Wonderful Life.*

Lee

It's a good thing we began rehearsing in October, because getting twenty-seven UU's together for anything is a challenge comparable to herding cats! Rehearsals were Sundays right after the church service. We were blessed with professional-quality readings by Richard Albright as Henry Potter and by Jerry Fitzmaurice as Clarence, the angel. We gave two "performances" (readings with a few props and appropriate clothing) on a Sunday before Christmas – at Sky Island UU church in the morning, Mountain View Gardens in the afternoon.

When Richard suggested the Playreaders do selections from Edgar Lee Masters' *Spoon River Anthology* we were enthusiastic. Richard did the planning and the directing. He assigned ten of us four characters each to memorize. The cast dressed in period, funeral, or ghostly attire; and the performances got rave reviews at both church and Mountain View Gardens.

I hope we aren't done.

Birthing *Imagine*

When the three months' of rehearsals and two performances of *It's a Wonderful Life* were done, I feared a letdown and figured I needed another project.

Looking around our small (90-member?) congregation, I realized there were some really talented members. I proposed we put together a Sky Island creative writing anthology. Well! The response was so overwhelming that the editors, Lorraine Groberg, Chris Braswell, and I, had to tell the prose writers to go do their own thing. And we had to limit the poetry writers to twenty poems each.

It was a labor of love; in fact, it took nine months to gestate. We went for quality in paper and cover, and *Imagine* made its debut in December 2015 at a big gala at the church. Within a month or so, sales had already covered the production costs so proceeds now go to the church.

Imagine is a handsome small volume with an attractive fractal design for the cover. It contains

Lee

one hundred poems by twenty different writers, twenty of which are mine. I'm probably prejudiced, but, in a way, *Imagine* is my baby.

Let me know if you'd like a copy.

Acknowledgments

My daughter Hillary Lee did the cover drawing of the Chambered Nautilus shell which is repeated inside at chapter headings.

Judy Visty and Jean MacKeen read some chapters early on and offered valuable suggestions.

Gary Lawrence did an exhaustive and constructive, criticism of the first chapter.

Daughter Lisa Lee read the entire manuscript and reminded me of some critical omissions.

Lorraine Groberg did meticulous read-throughs with both early and late drafts. Her many suggestions have resulted in significant improvements in *Reflections*.

Grateful thanks to Kerry Hales, technical guru, who taught me some useful skills and frequently had to convince my computer to behave.

Lee

Special thanks to Chris G. Braswell who edited and formatted the manuscript and made the arrangements to get *Reflections* into print.

I owe a particular debt of gratitude to the Writers' Interest Group of Mountain View Gardens, who patiently listened to me read chapters from the work in progress. Many of the happenings, reminiscences, and musings set forth in *Reflections* came about because I felt the need to write something for our Tuesday morning meetings.